BE MY VALENTINE

HUGS & KISSES

4

I Love Cookies!

- **Thanksgiving Vest** — Paint designs (pg. 114) on purchased canvas vest. Use paper-backed fusible web to fuse fabric to lapels. Sew buttons and bows to vest.
- **Table Runner** — Paint designs (pg. 118) on fabric. Secure painted design to purchased table runner using paper-backed fusible web. Glue ribbon along edges.
- **Basket** — Paint design (pg. 112) on fabric and follow Making a Padded Shape (pg. 170). Hot glue padded shape to side of basket. Tie raffia bow around handle.

- **Christmas Bib** — Paint designs (pg. 159). Add details using dimensional fabric paint. Add words using black permanent pen. Sew rickrack to bib.
- **Santa Sweatshirt** — Paint design (pg. 124). Add details using dimensional glitter fabric paint. Sew buttons and bows to sweatshirt.
- **Christmas Dress** — Paint designs (pgs. 133 and 134). Sew ribbon bow to dress.
- **Ornaments** — Color designs (pg. 158) on bristol board; cut out. Punch hole in top of design; hang with ribbon.
- **Nutcracker Boxes** — Paint designs (pg. 125) on bristol board; cut out. Glue to painted papier-mâché boxes. Glue sheet music to lids. Embellish with ribbons, gold cording, and bells.

GENERAL INSTRUCTIONS

TRANSFERRING DESIGNS

Before transferring your design, use a small test transfer included in the book on a scrap of fabric or paper similar to your project to help you determine the best iron temperature and length of time needed to achieve a good transfer.

1. If you are transferring a design to a fabric item that will be washed, first wash and dry the item without using fabric softener; press.
2. Preheat the iron for five minutes on appropriate setting for item being used. Do **not** use steam.
3. Because transfer ink may bleed through fabric, protect ironing board cover by placing a clean piece of fabric or paper on cover.
4. (*Note: The inked transfer is the reverse of what will appear.*) Place transfer, **inked side down** on **right side** of fabric or paper. Place iron on the transfer; hold for five seconds. Do **not** slide iron. Pick up iron and move to another position on transfer so areas under steam holes are transferred. Carefully lift one corner of transfer to see if design has been transferred to item. If not, place iron on transfer a few more seconds.

Alternate method for transferring to dark item:
Trace design onto tracing paper. Place dressmaker's tracing paper, coated side down, on right side of item. Place traced design, right side down, on dressmaker's tracing paper. Use a stylus or a dull pencil to draw over lines of design.

PAINTING DESIGNS

1. Stabilize fabric by ironing freezer paper (coated side toward fabric) to wrong side under design area. Place a waxed T-shirt form or a piece of plastic-wrapped cardboard beneath fabric; secure fabric with T-pins.
2. Test a fine-point permanent pen on a hidden area of your item to make sure ink does not bleed. Draw over all outlines and detail lines with pen. If you cover some detail lines when painting, lines can be redrawn after paint is completely dry.
3. If painting on bristol board or an item that will not be washed, use acrylic paint. If item will be washed, use fabric paint or a mixture of half textile medium and half acrylic paint.
4. Some project designs were shaded. To shade an area, dampen brush with water; dip one corner of brush into a darker paint. Stroke brush on a palette a few times to blend. Apply paint along outline of an area using one stroke.
5. Add outlines and detail lines using a fine-point permanent pen or a liner paintbrush and paint.
6. Follow paint manufacturer's instructions to heat-set and launder.

COLORING DESIGNS

1. Use colored pencils to color design. To prevent smudging, color design from top to bottom.
2. Use a fine-point permanent pen to draw over all lines of design.
3. For a shaded look, color design lighter in the center of an area and darker around the edges.
4. Seal projects with workable fixative spray.

Continued on pg. 170.

Art by Anne Fetzer

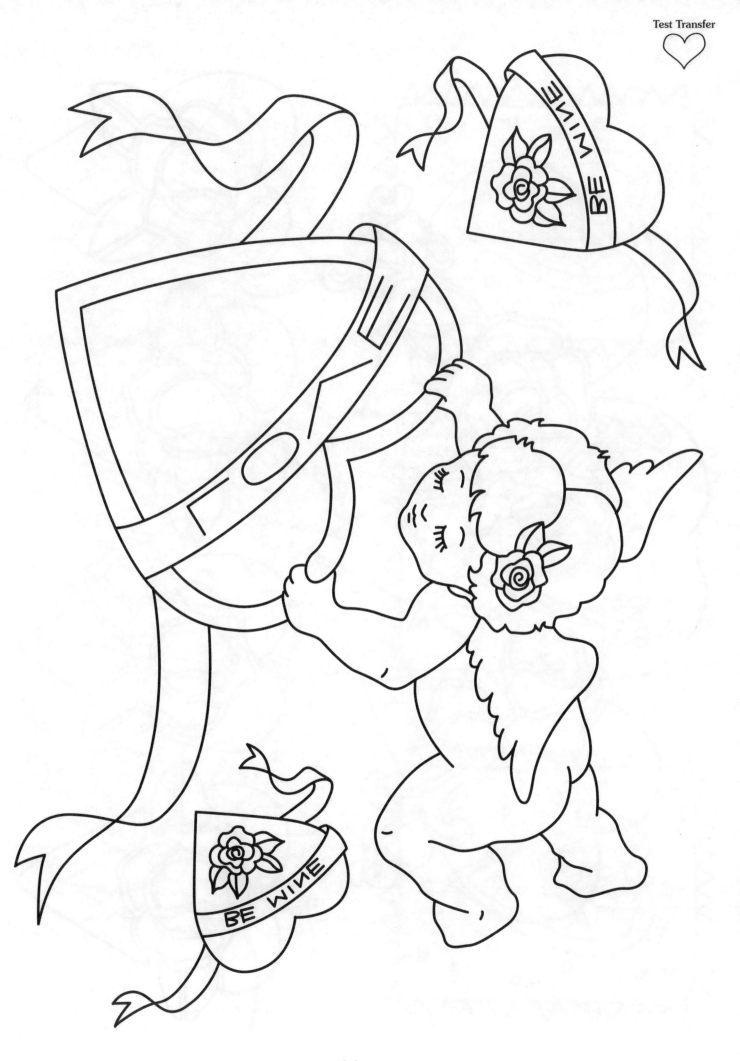

Art by Anne Fetzer

Art by Anne Freuw

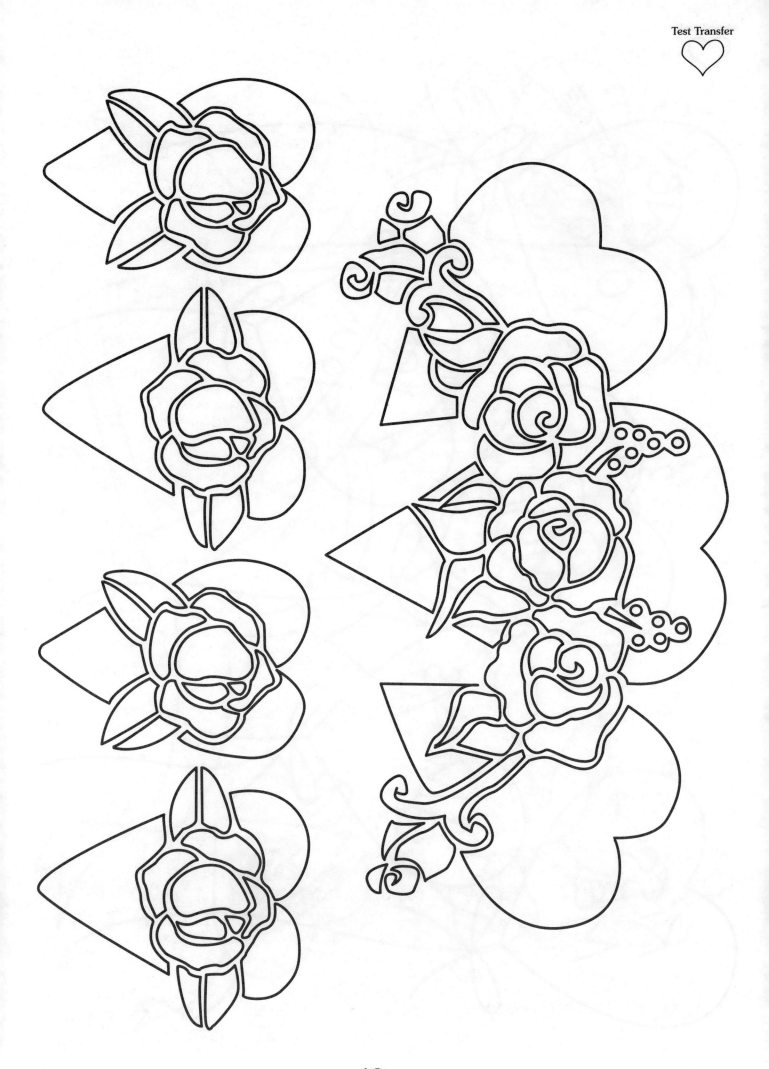

12

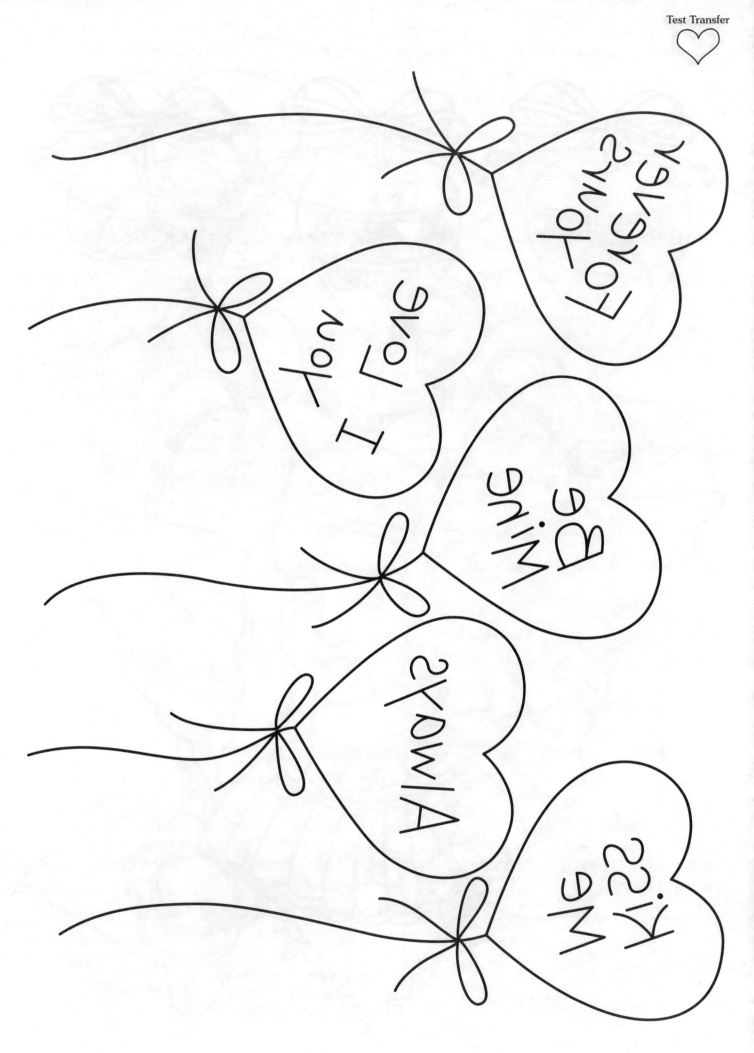

BE LIEVE IN A LITTLE MAGIC

Art by Anne Fetzer

...love bears all things

Art by Kathie Rueger

Art by Anne Fetzer

Be Mine

Art by Anne Fetzer

rt by Vicky Howard

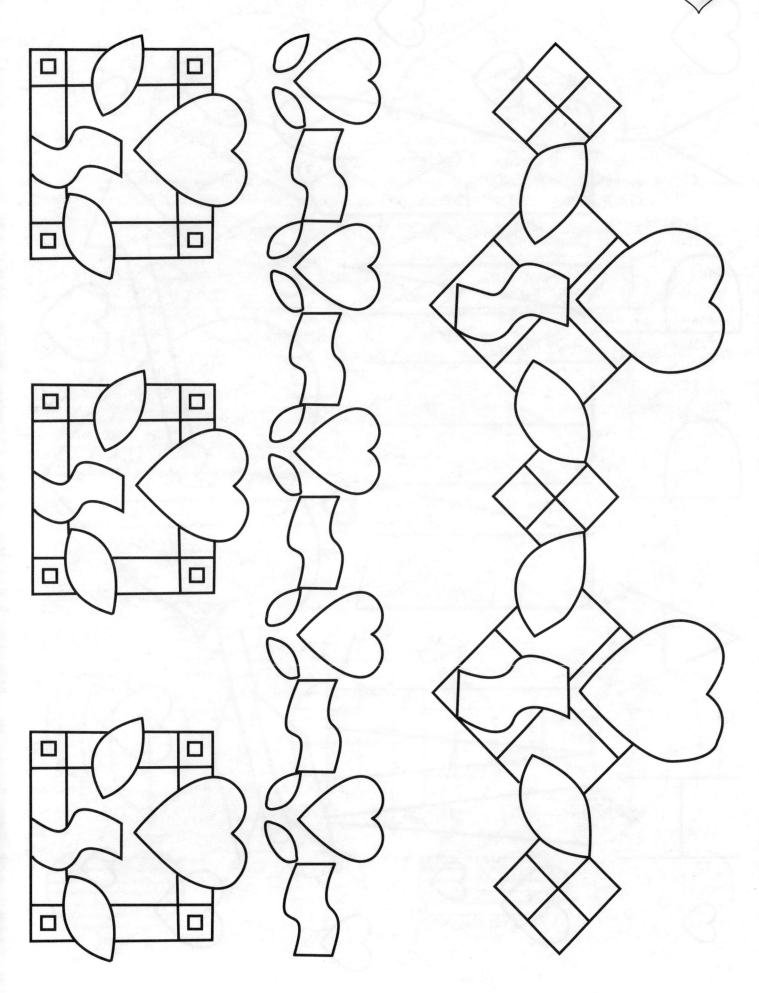

Art by Anne Fetzer

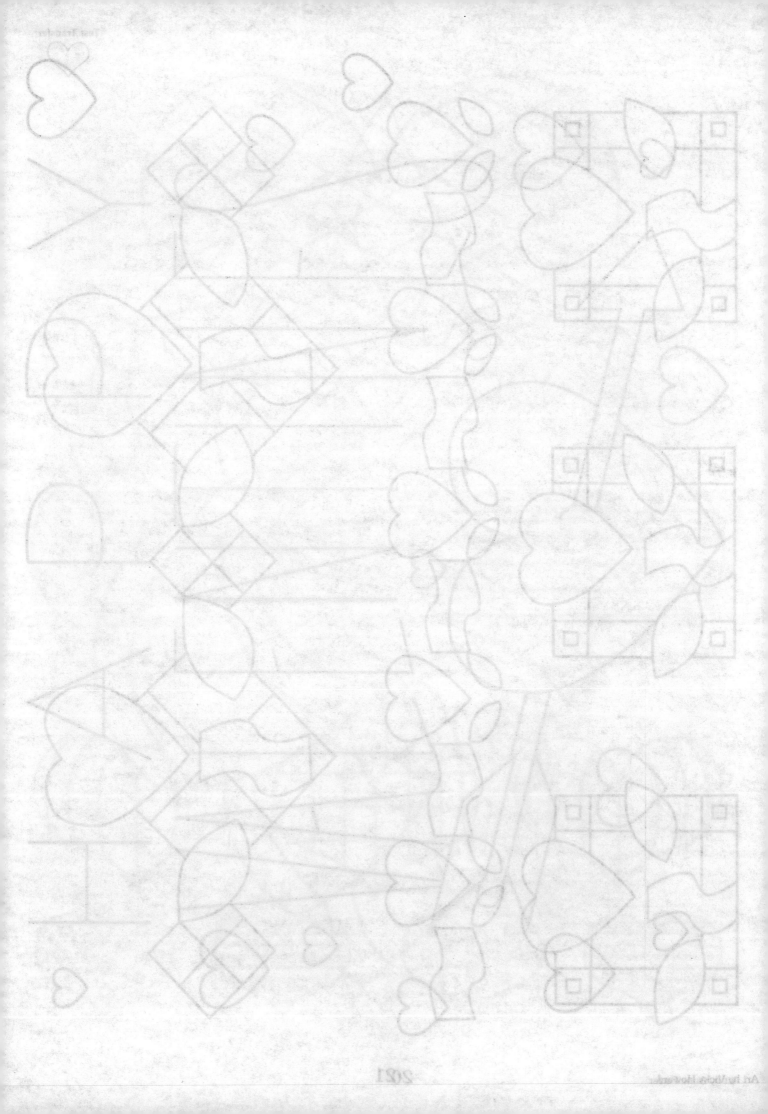

21

23

Art by Anne Fetzer

Art by Anne Fetzer

25

Art by Gerri Sorkin

26

Art by Anne Fetzer

29

Art by Vicky Howard

30

Art by Gerri Sorkin

Welcome it! Xc pe Meghin, areen

Beary Irish!

Art by Kathie Rueger

Art by Anne Fetzer

easter buddies

Art by Anne Fetzer

Test Transfer

Art by Anne Fetzer

40

Art by Anne Fetzer

41

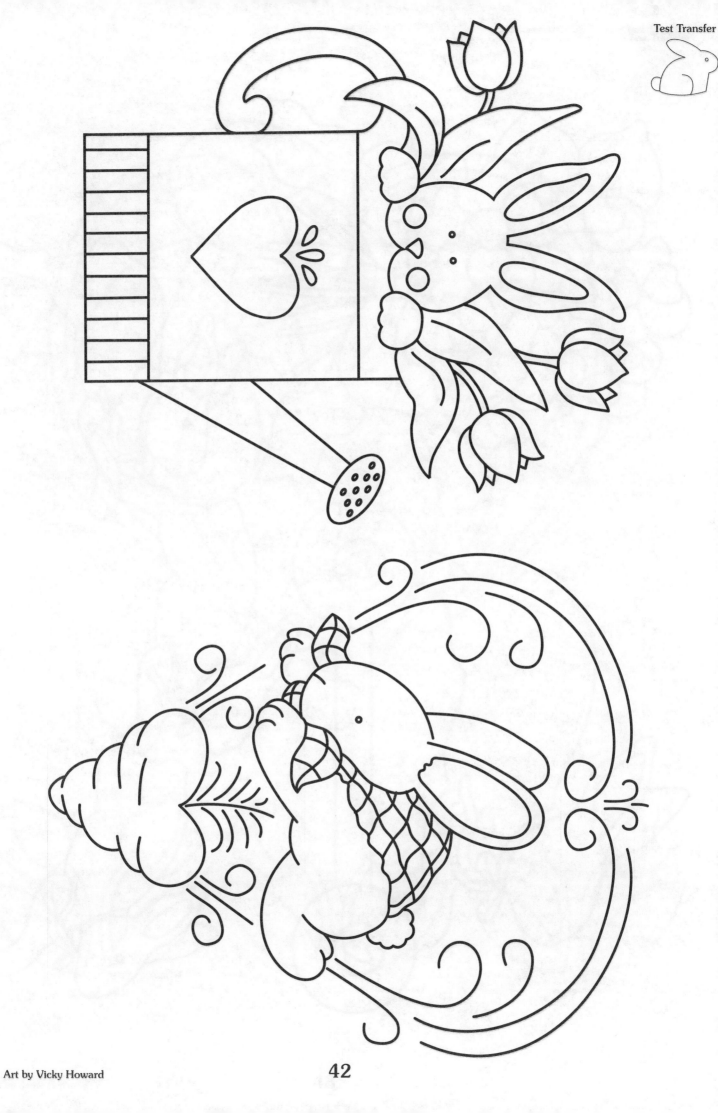

Art by Vicky Howard

43

Art by Vicky Howard

SPRING TIME

FRESH

HARE

Art by Vicky Howard

Art by Vicky Howard

50

Art by Anne Fetzer

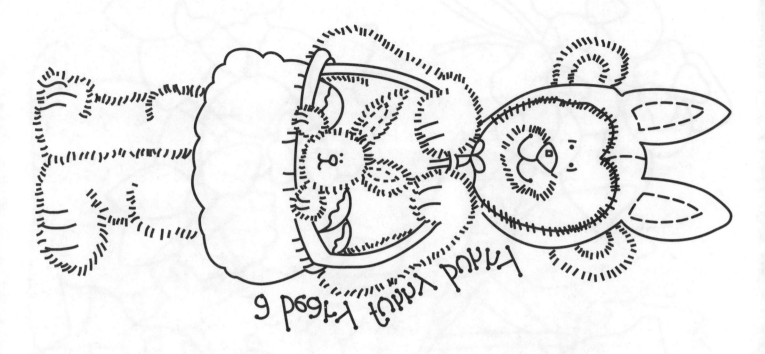

some bunny loves u

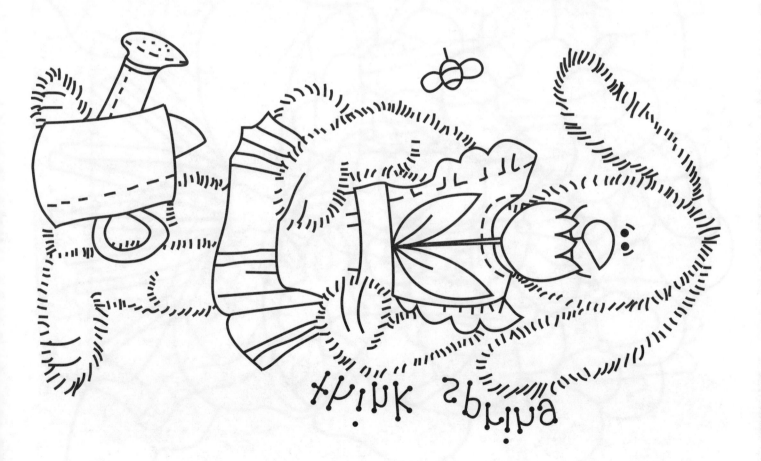

think spring

Art by Kathie Rueger

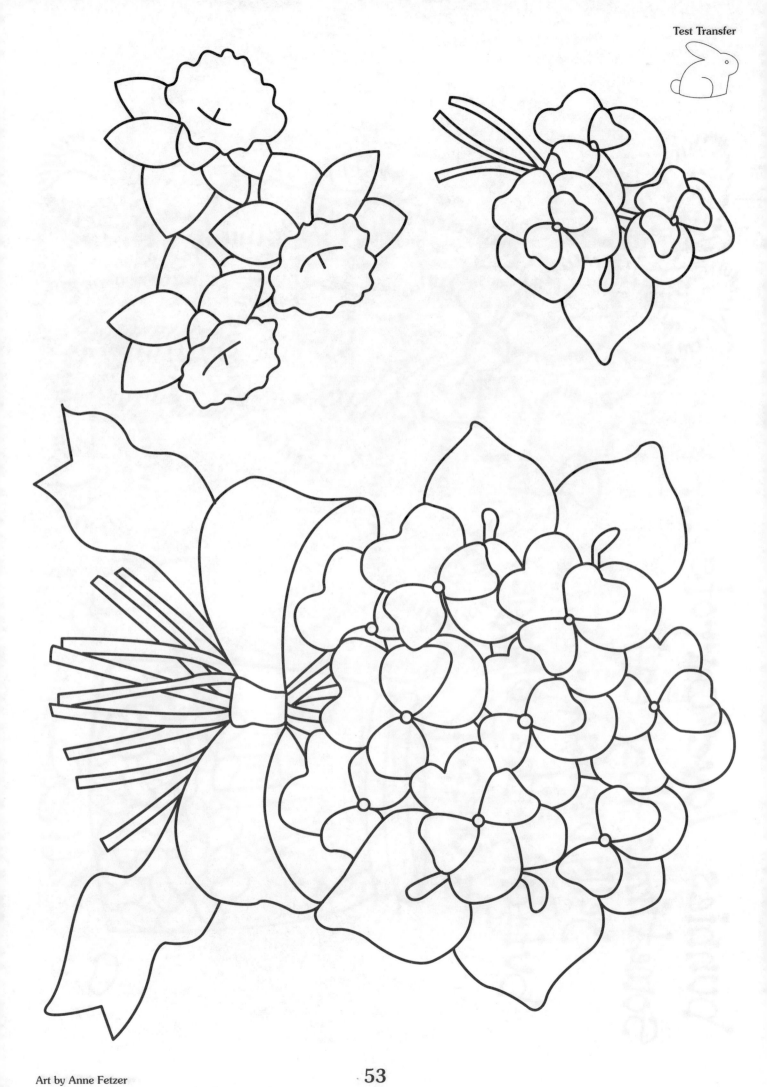

53

bunnies love carrots
sometimes

Bunnies love carrots...

sometimes they eat...

Jelly beans...

but only the orange ones...

Art by Kathie Rueger

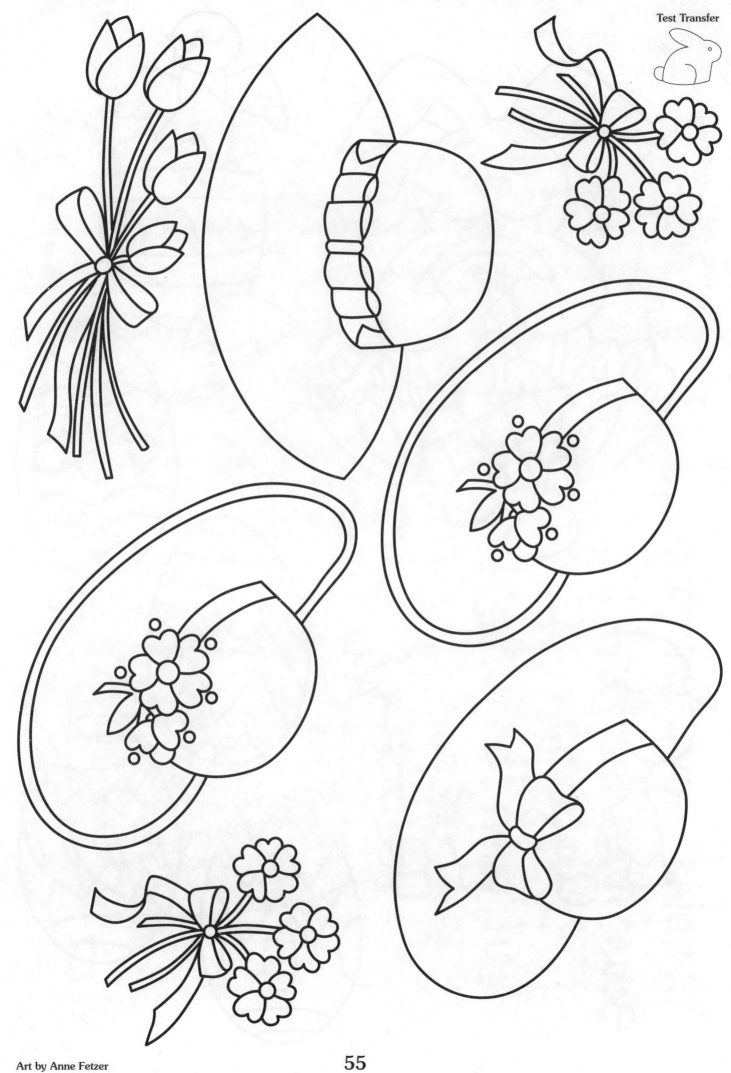

Art by Anne Fetzer

Art by Gerri Sorkin

56

57

Art by Anne Fetzer

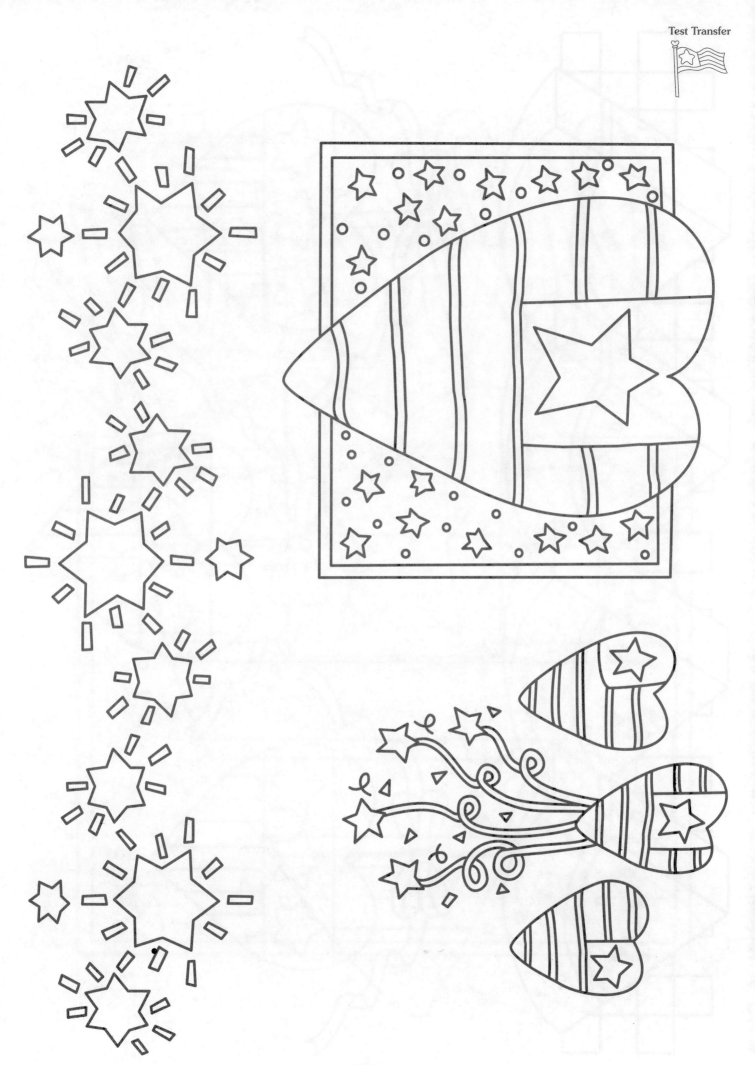

Art by Anne Fetzer

Art by Anne Forster

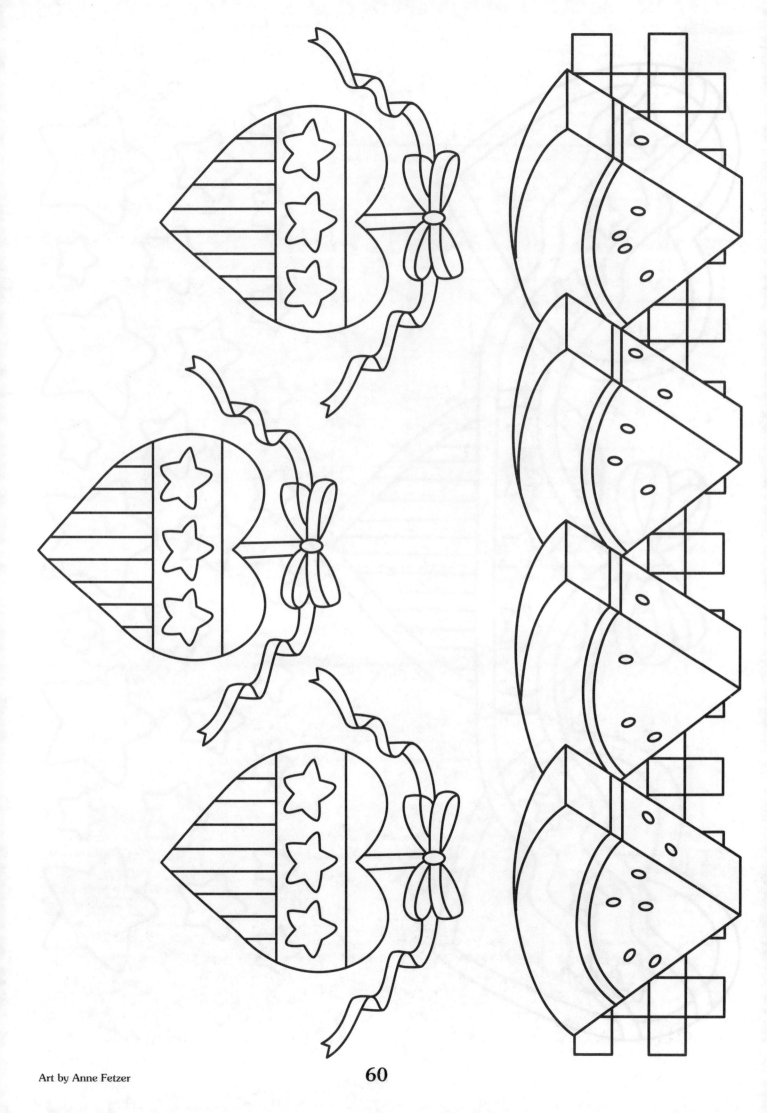

Art by Anne Fetzer

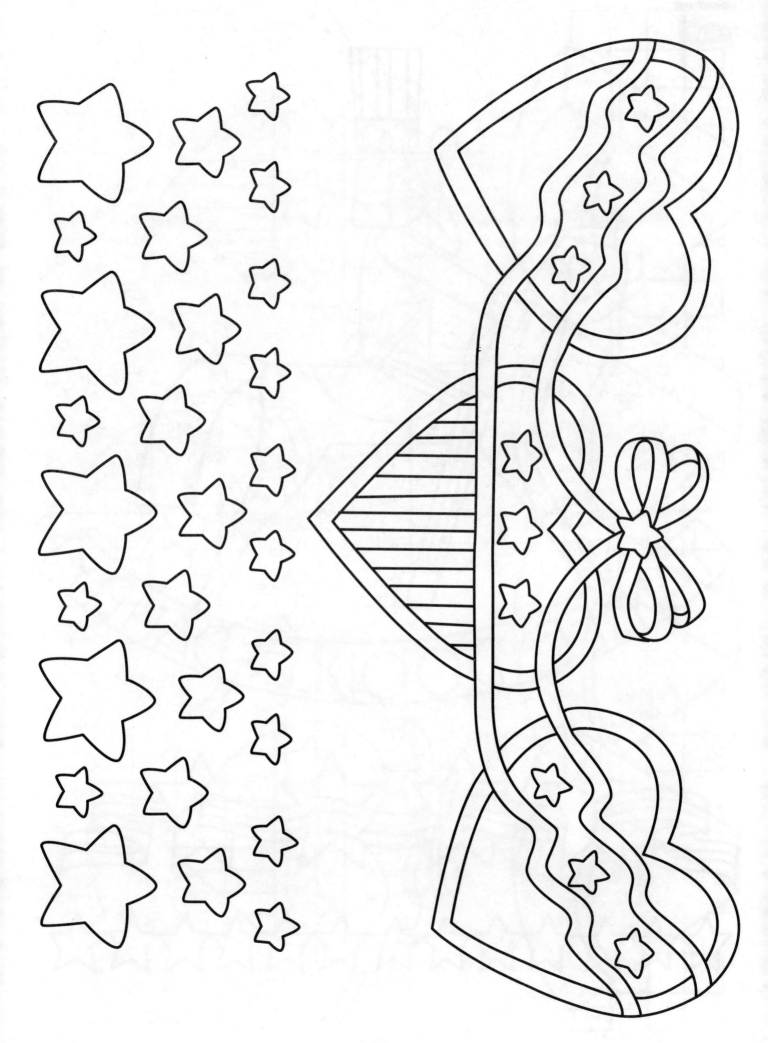

YANKEE DOODLE DANDY

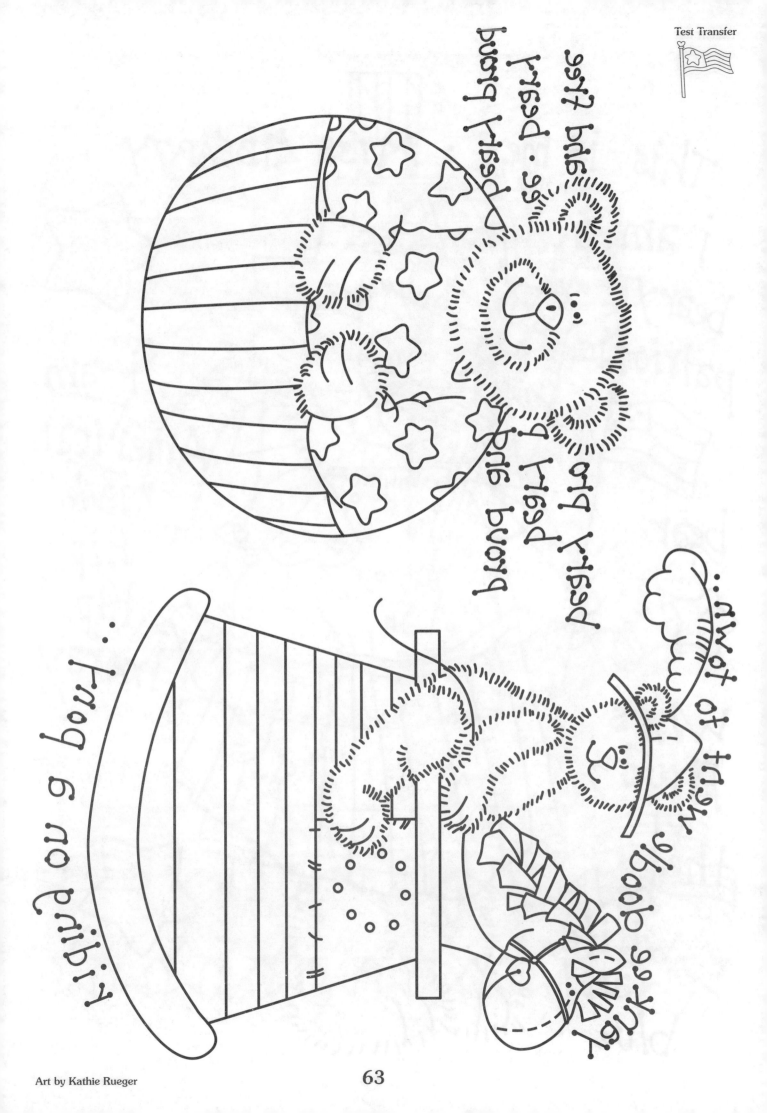

pearly proud and pearly free

pearly pro pearly proud and

pearly proud and pearly pro

...riding on a boat

...want to goodle go town

Art by Kathie Rueger

This is me

free

brave

proud

MISS LIBEARTY

i am a

beary

patriotic

i am

American

made

hip

hip

hooray

bear

who's

proud

of

the

red

white

and

blue

This is me • Miss LiBEARty

i am a beary patriotic bear

i am American made hip hip hip hooray

Who's proud of the red white and blue

Art by Kathie Rueger

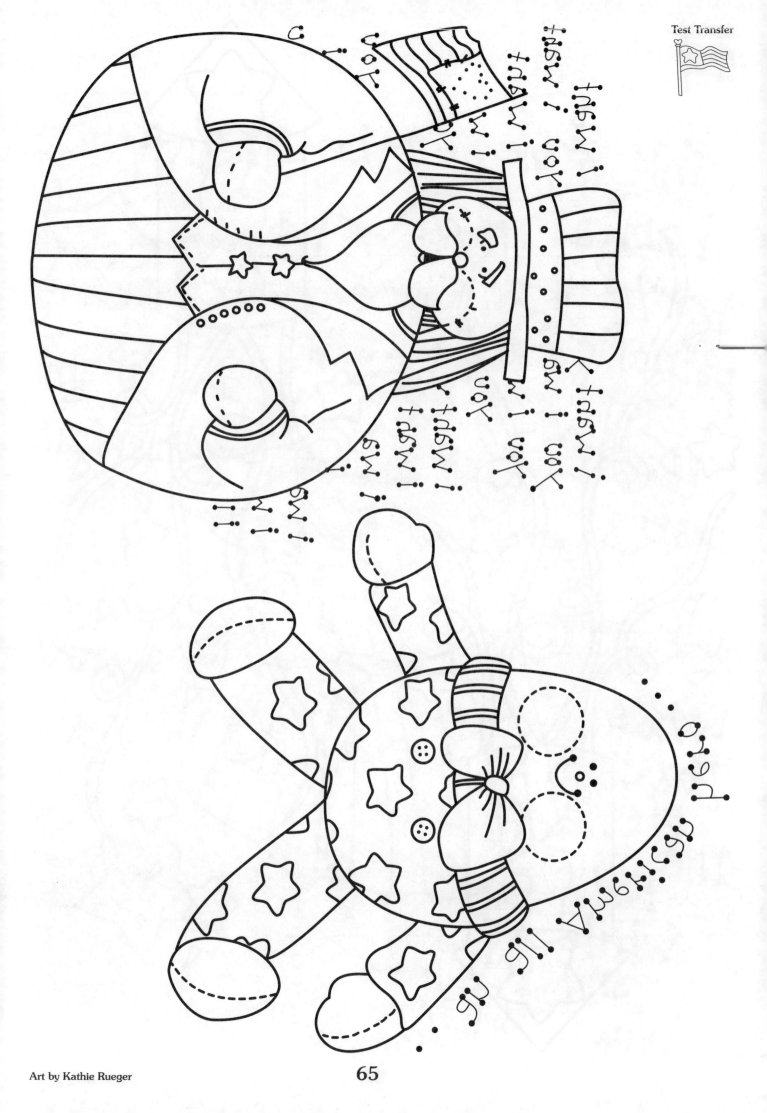

Art by Kathie Rueger

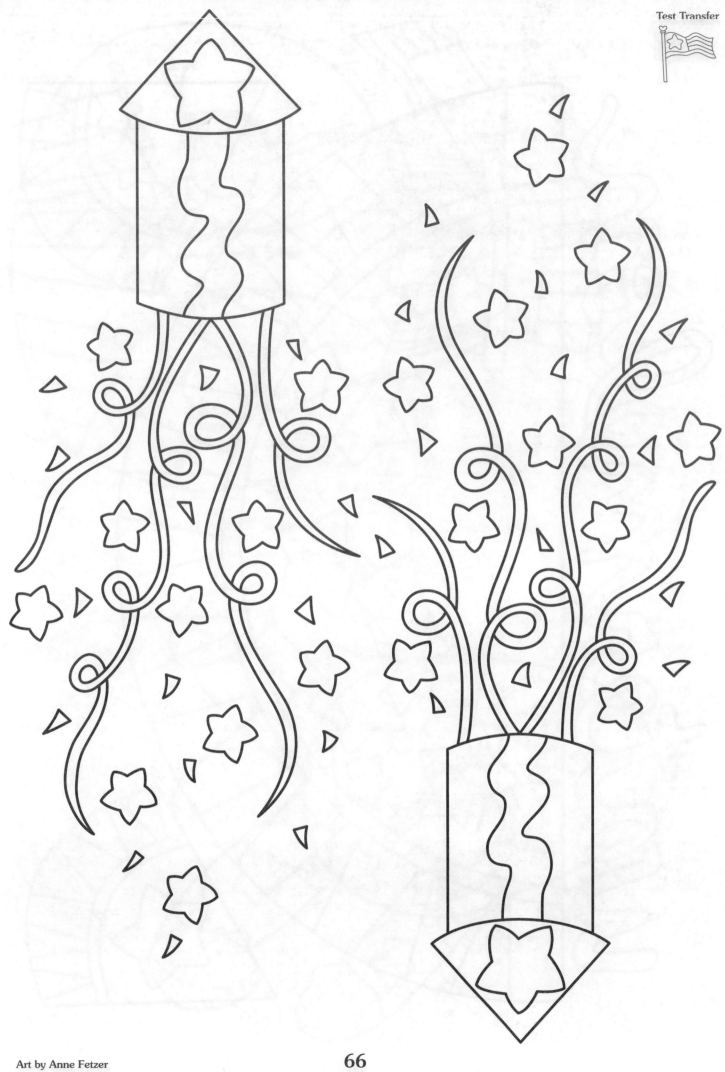

Art by Anne Fetzer

66

67

Art by Vicky Howard

Bless our Country

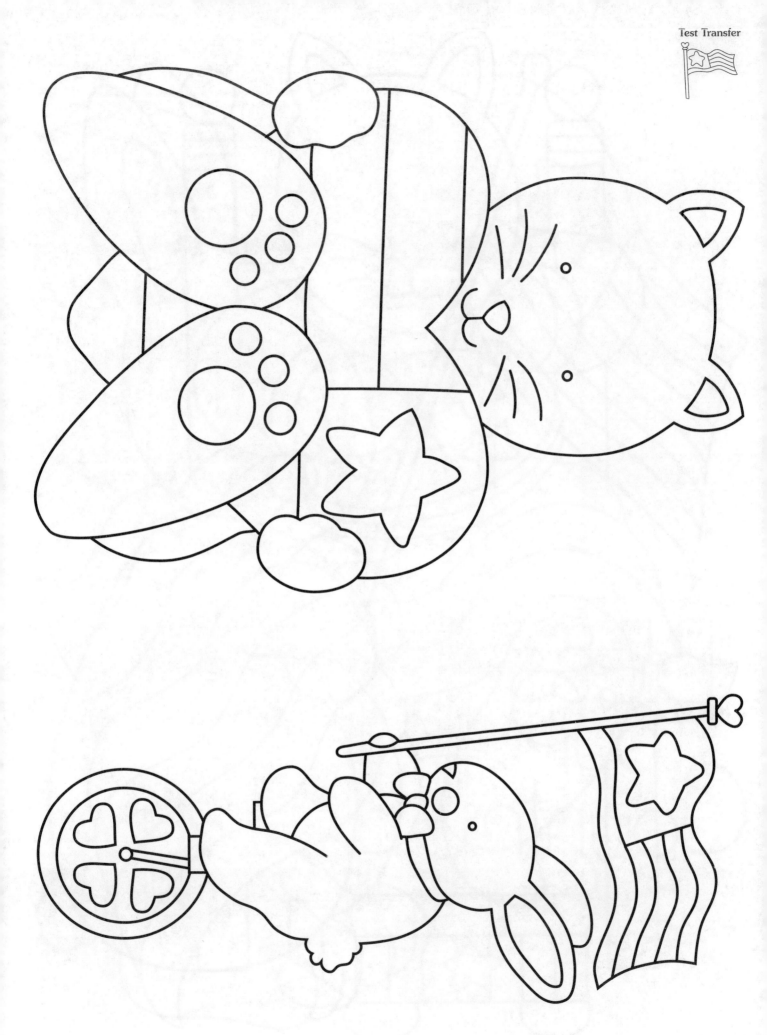

Art by Vicky Howard

Art by Anne Fetzer

Test Transfer

made in the

U.S.A.

HOMEGROWN

GOD BLESS

AMERICA

RED, WHITE AND BLUE

Art by Anne Fetzer

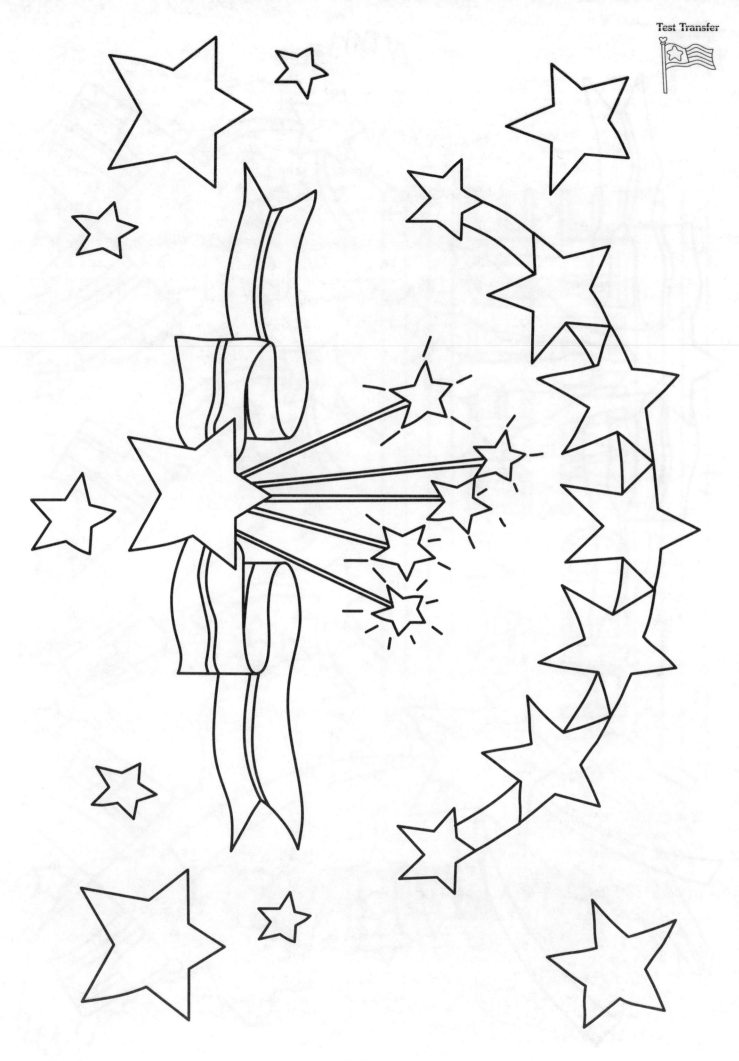

Art by Anne Fetzer

74

BOO

HAPPY HALLOWEEN

you a scaredy cat?

are you a scaredy cat?

Art by Kathie Rueger

Art by Kathie Rueger

Art by Vicky Howard

TRICK or TREAT

Art by Vicky Howard

Art by Anne Fetzer

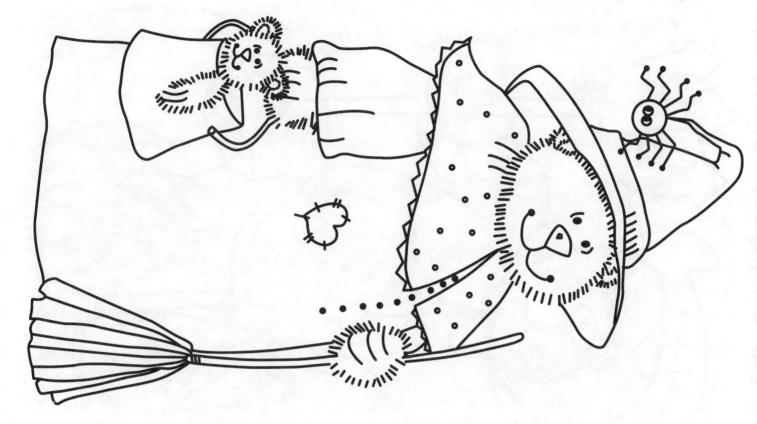

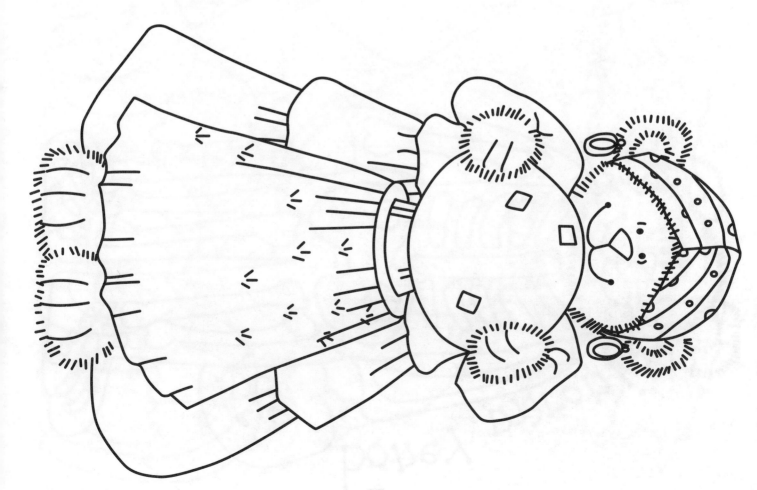

Art by Kathie Rueger

83

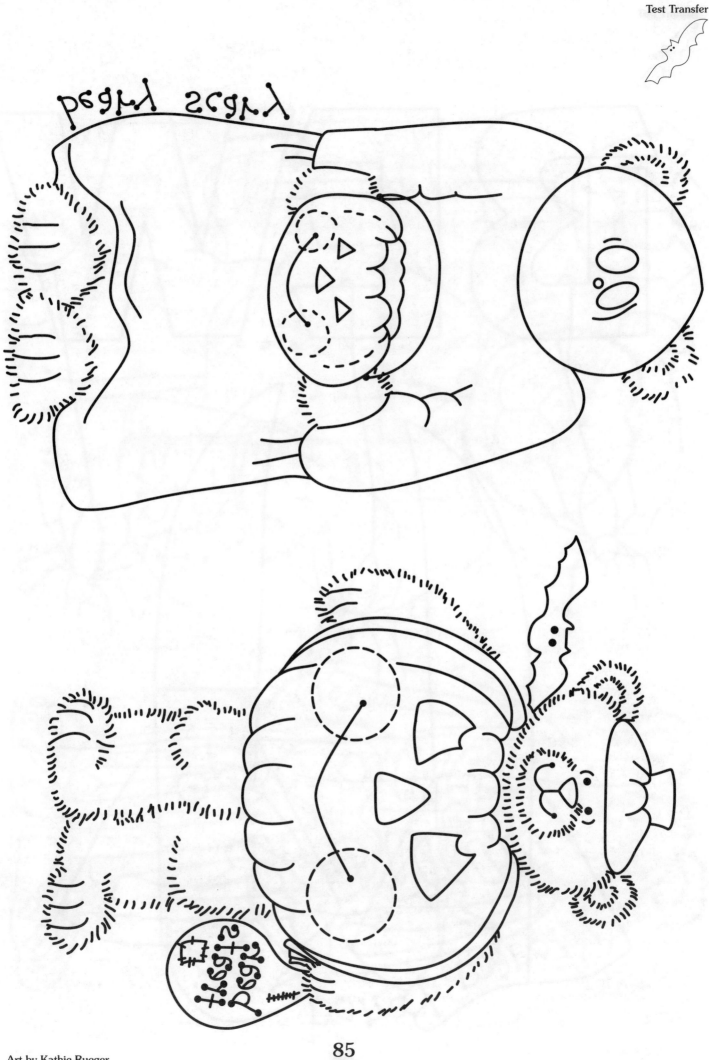

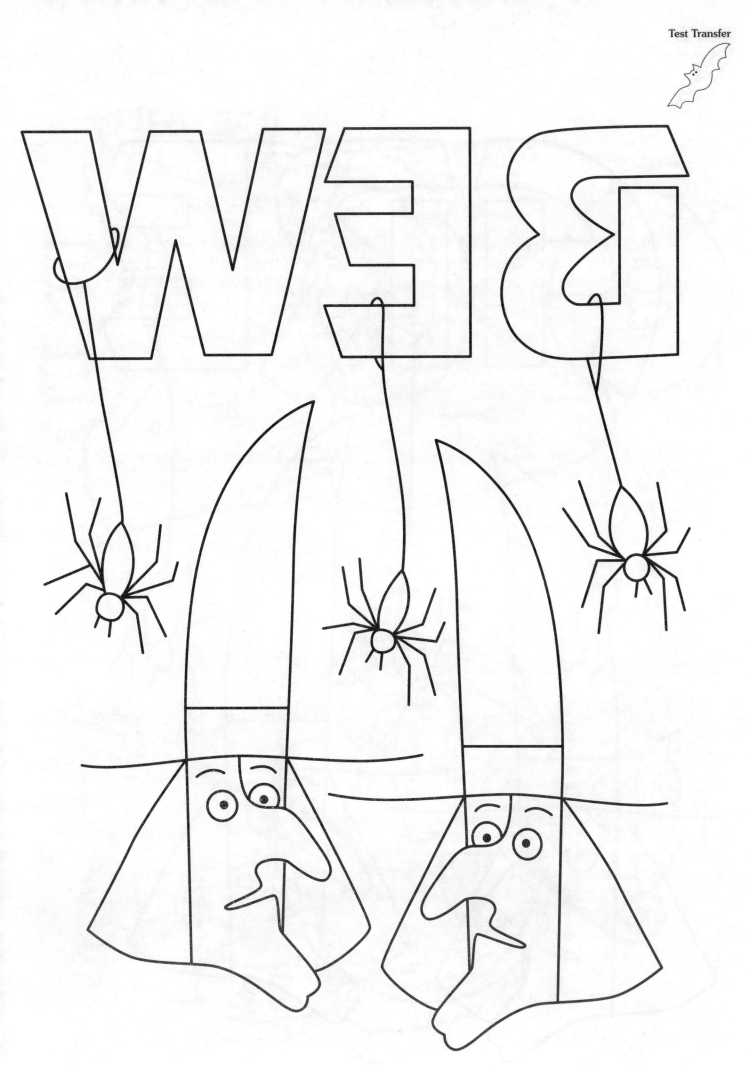

87

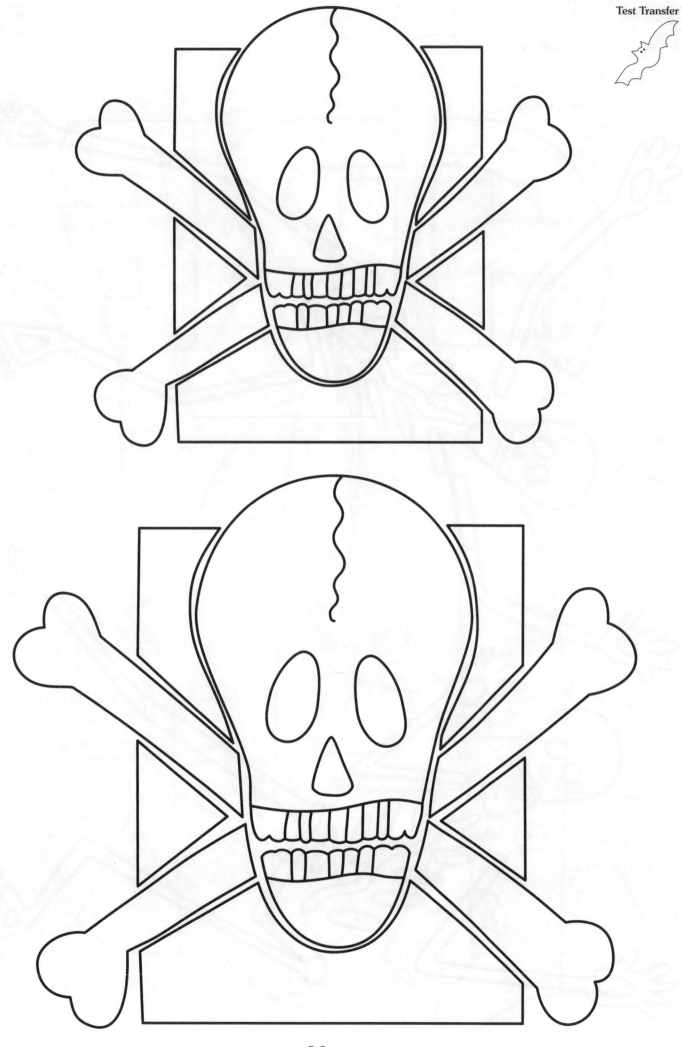

Art by Anne Fetzer

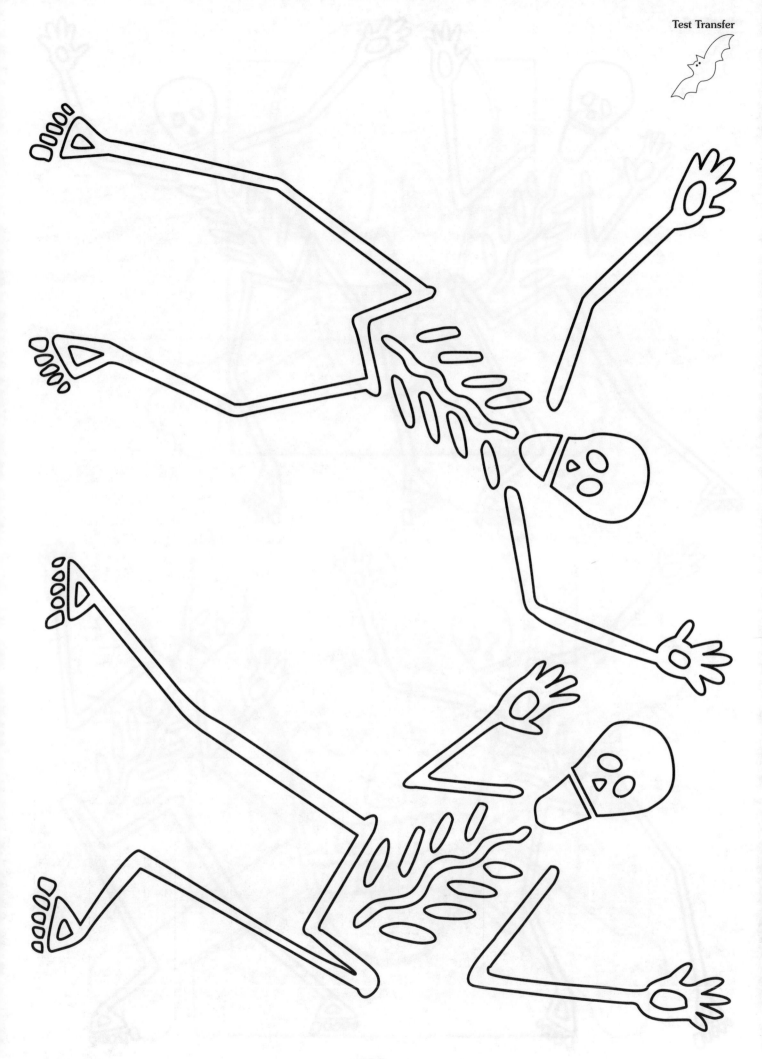

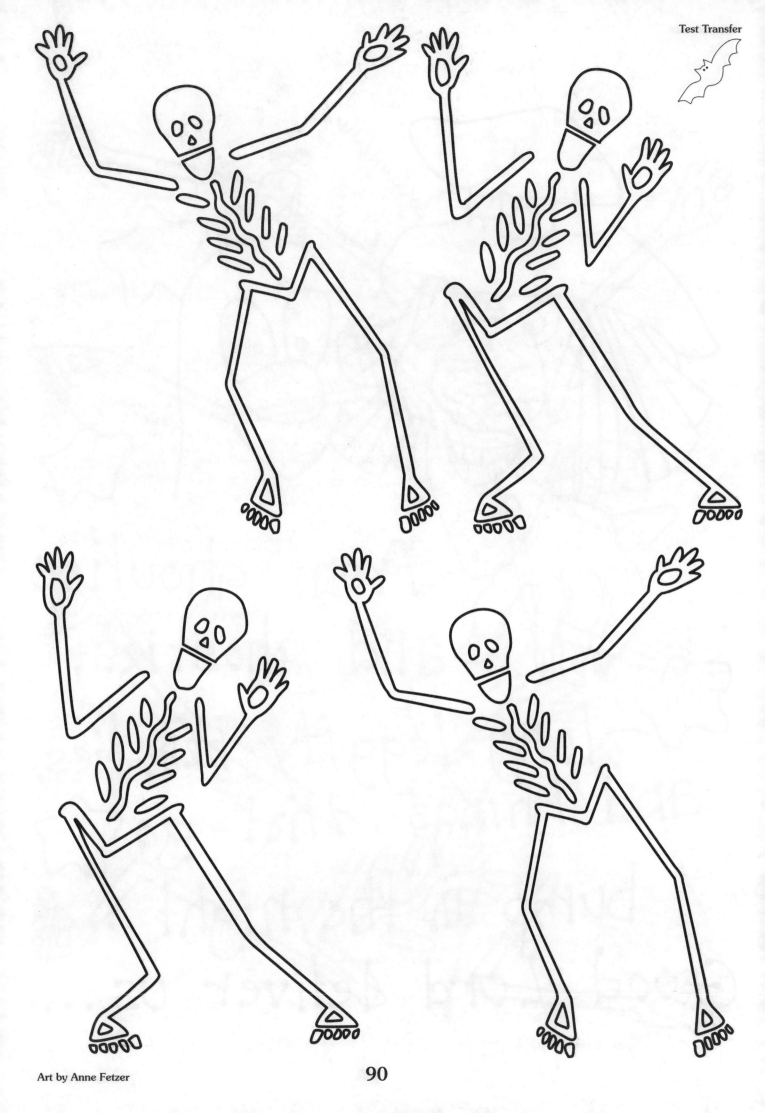

Art by Anne Fetzer

From ghoulies
and ghosties,
long-leggity beasties,
and things that go
... bump in the night
Good Lord deliver us ...

Test Transfer

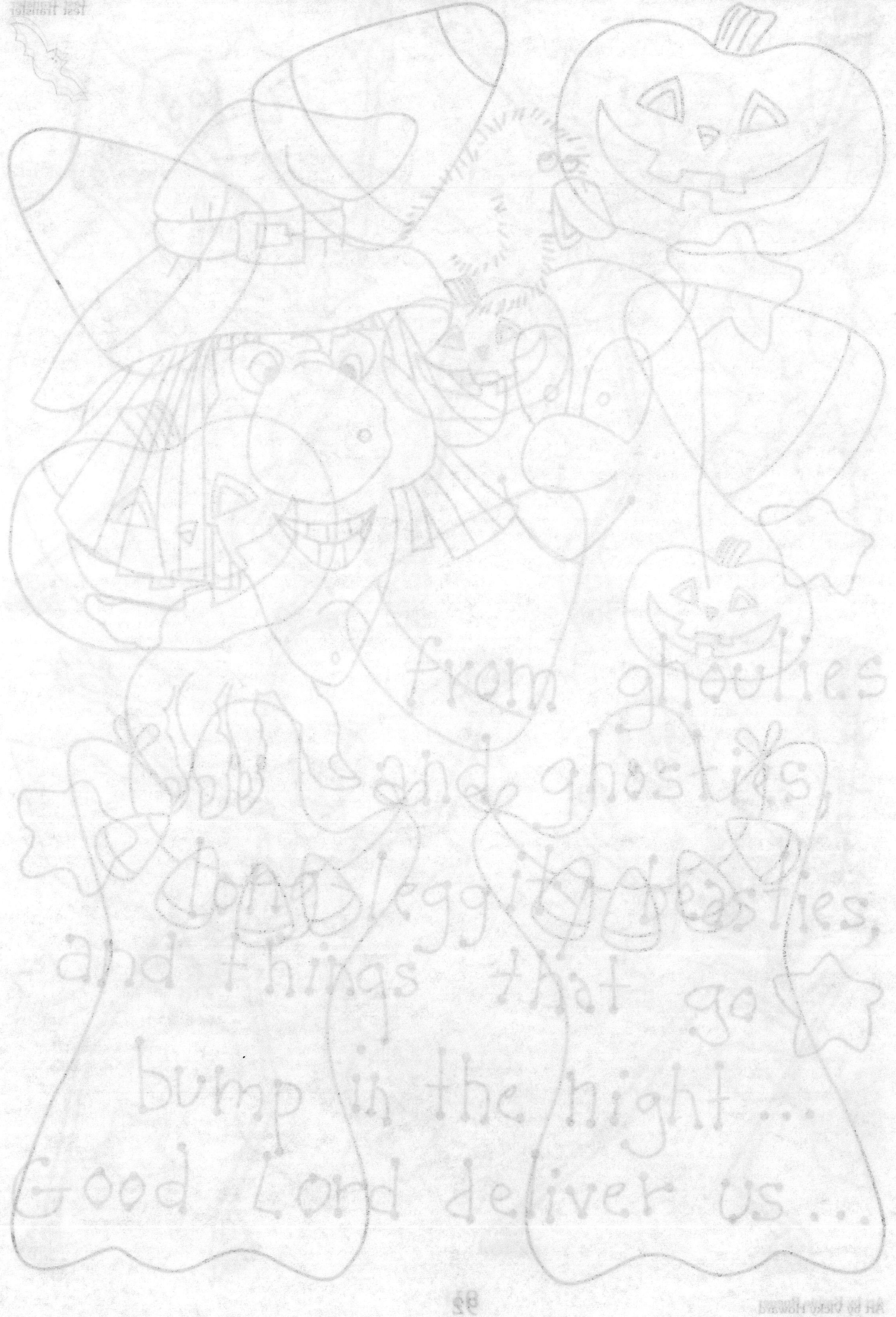
from ghoulies
and ghosties,
long leggity beasties,
and things that go
bump in the night...
Good Lord deliver us...

Art by Vicki Howard

Art by Vicky Howard

92

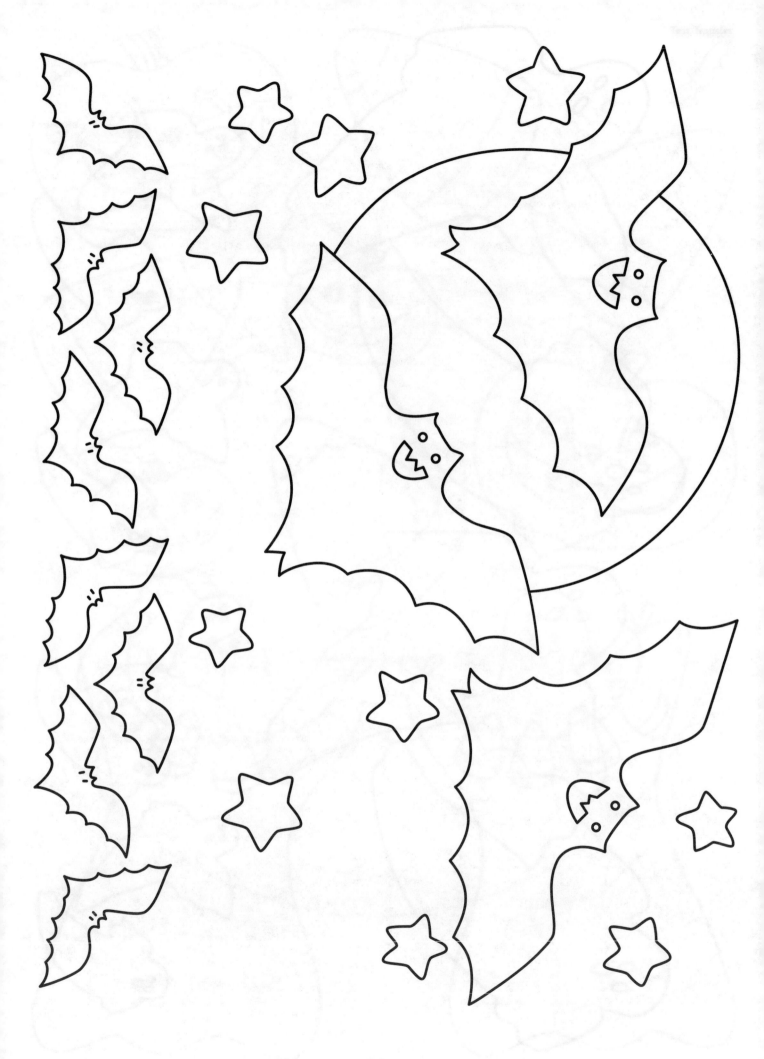

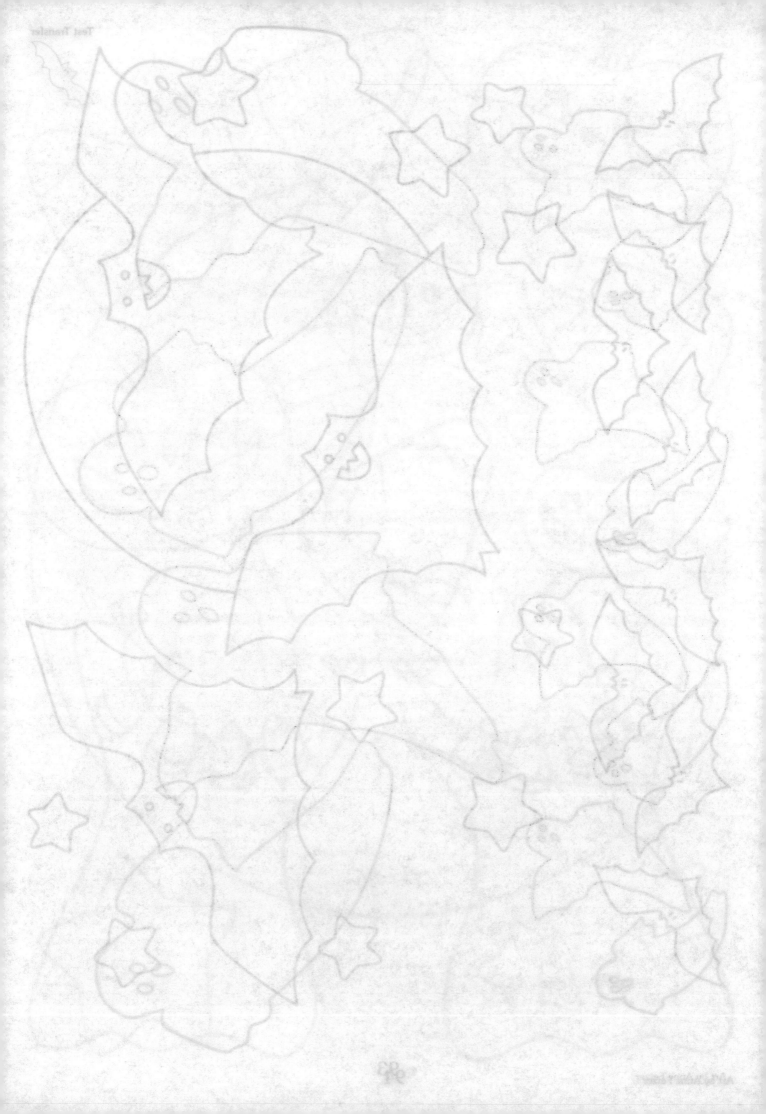

Art by Anne Fetzer

94

Art by Anne Fetzer

Art by Anne Fetzer

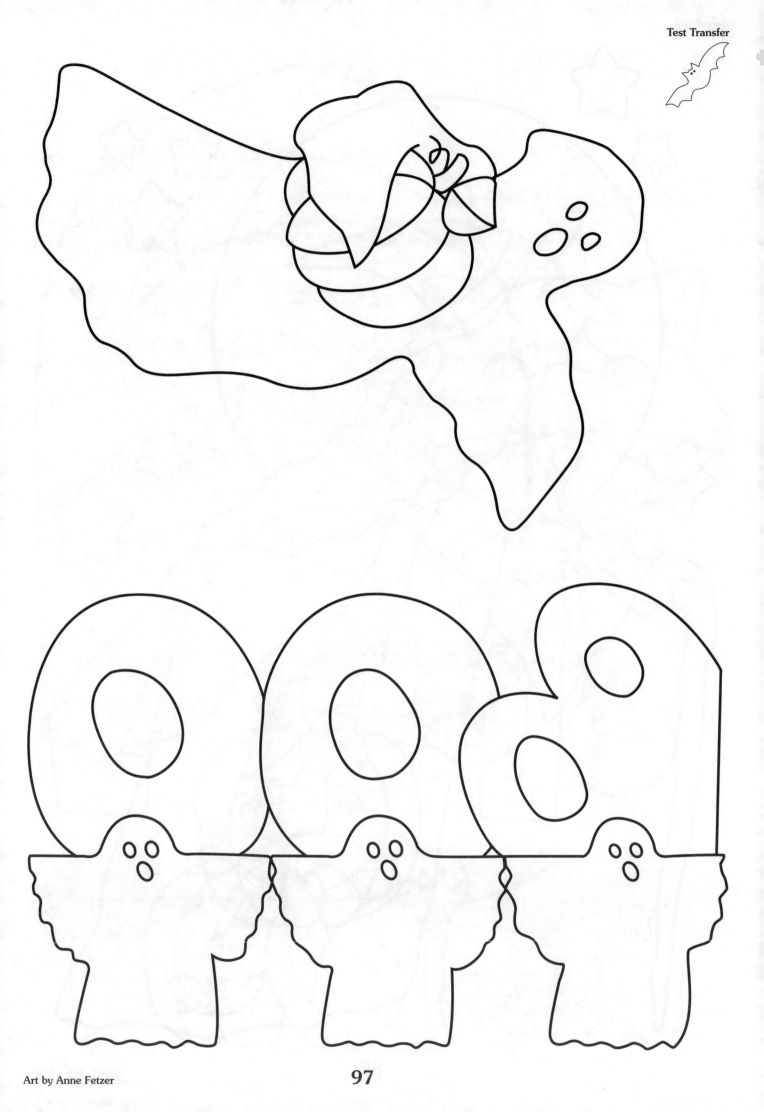

Art by Anne Fetzer

97

Art by Anne Fetzer

Trick or Treat

Art by Vicky Howard

Art by Vicky Howard

103

Art by Kathie Rueger

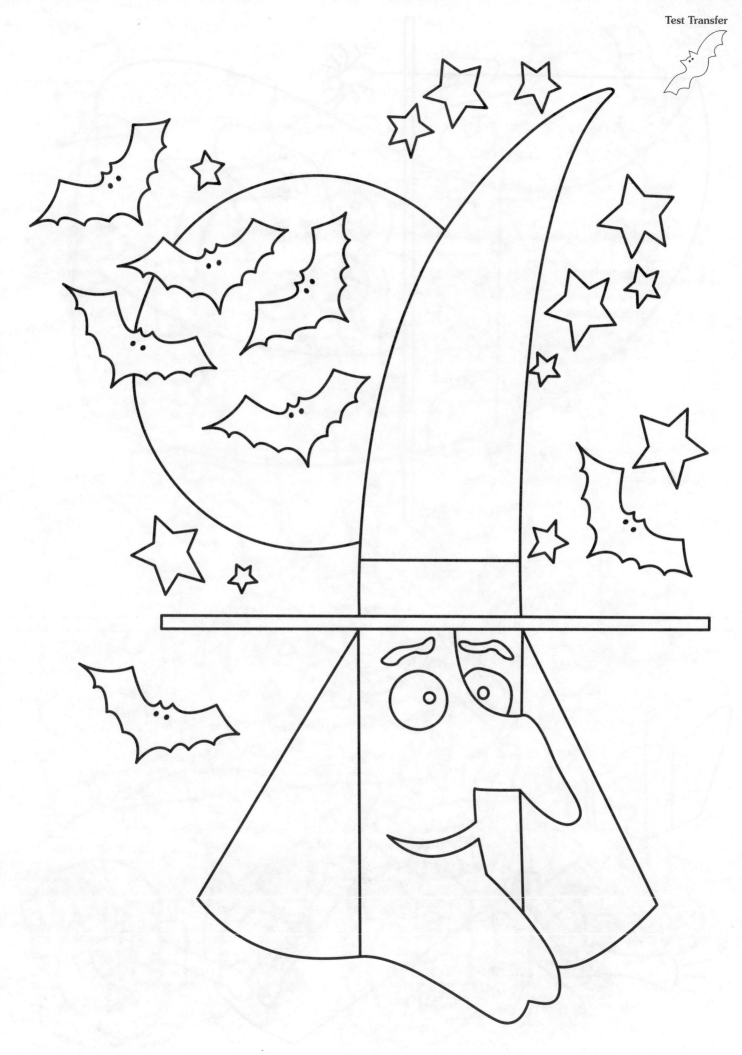

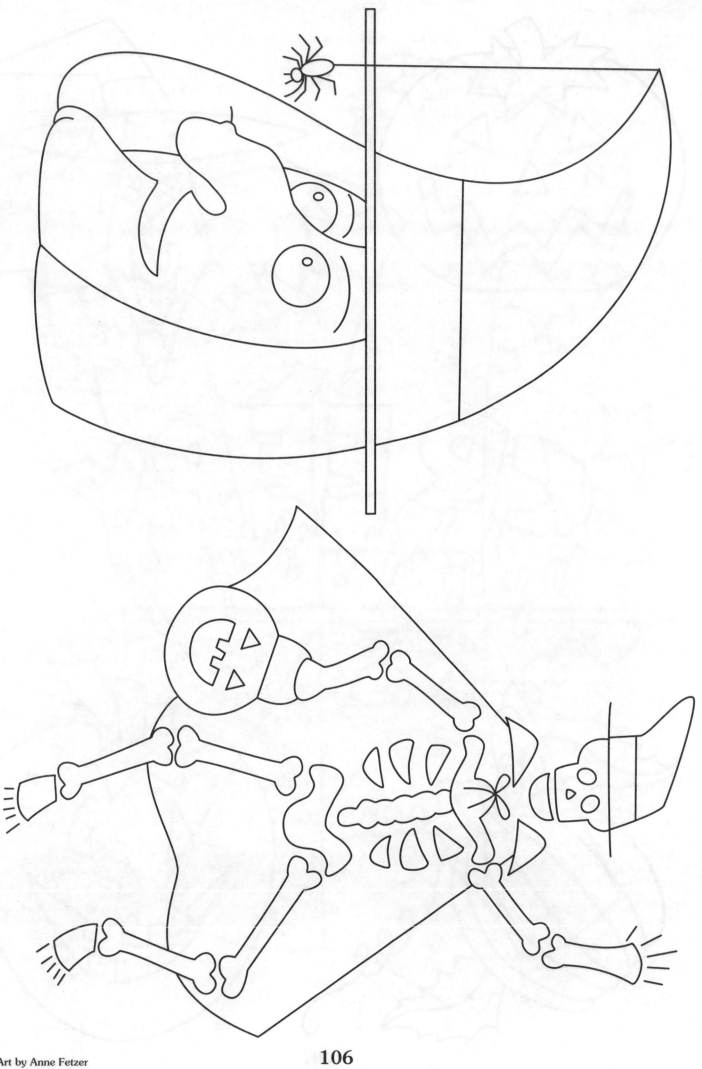

Art by Anne Fetzer

Art by Gerri Sorkin

Art by Gerri Sorkin

PUMPKIN PATCH

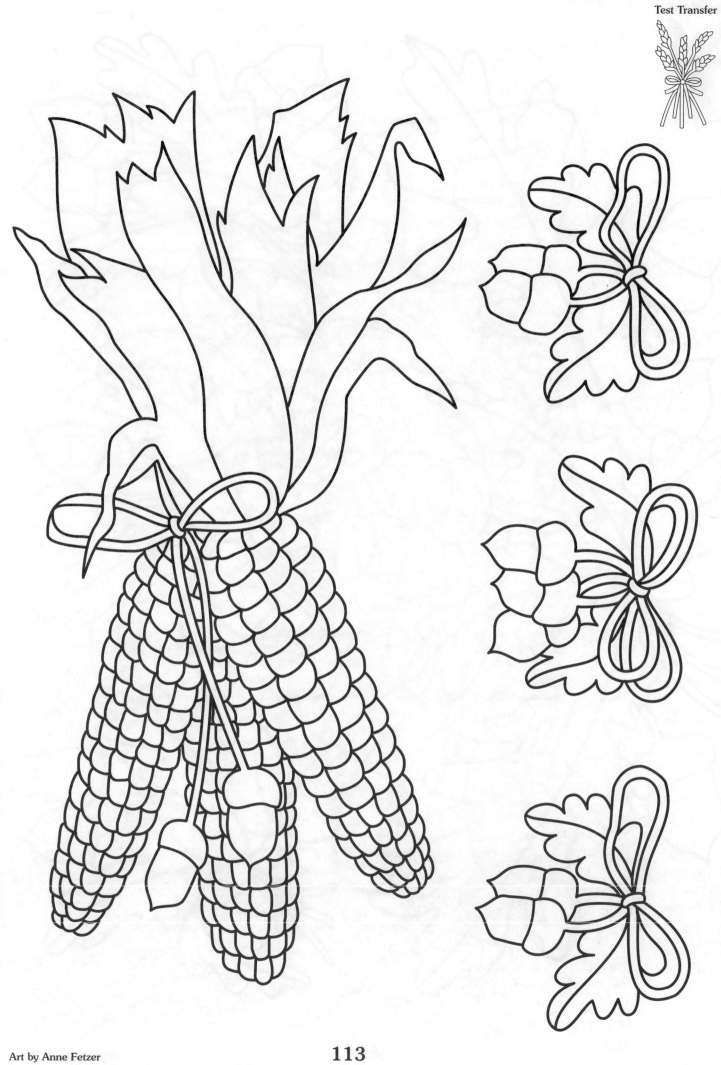

Art by Anne Fetzer

113

Art by Anne Fetzer

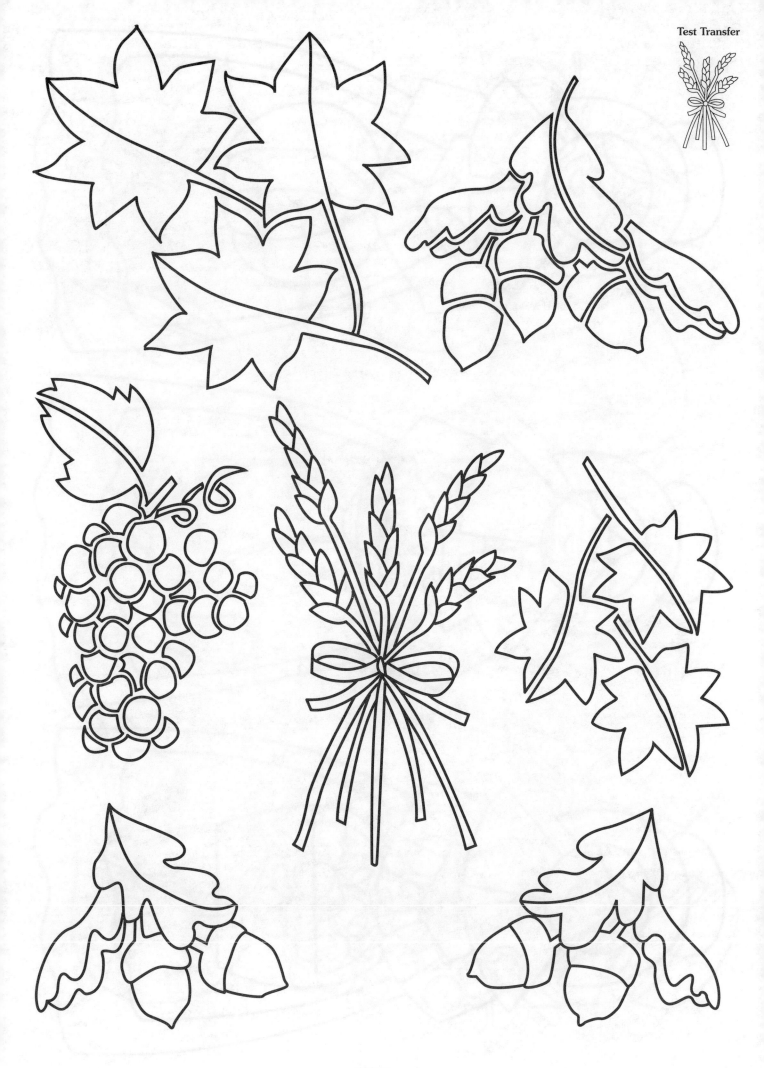

Art by Anne Fetzer

117

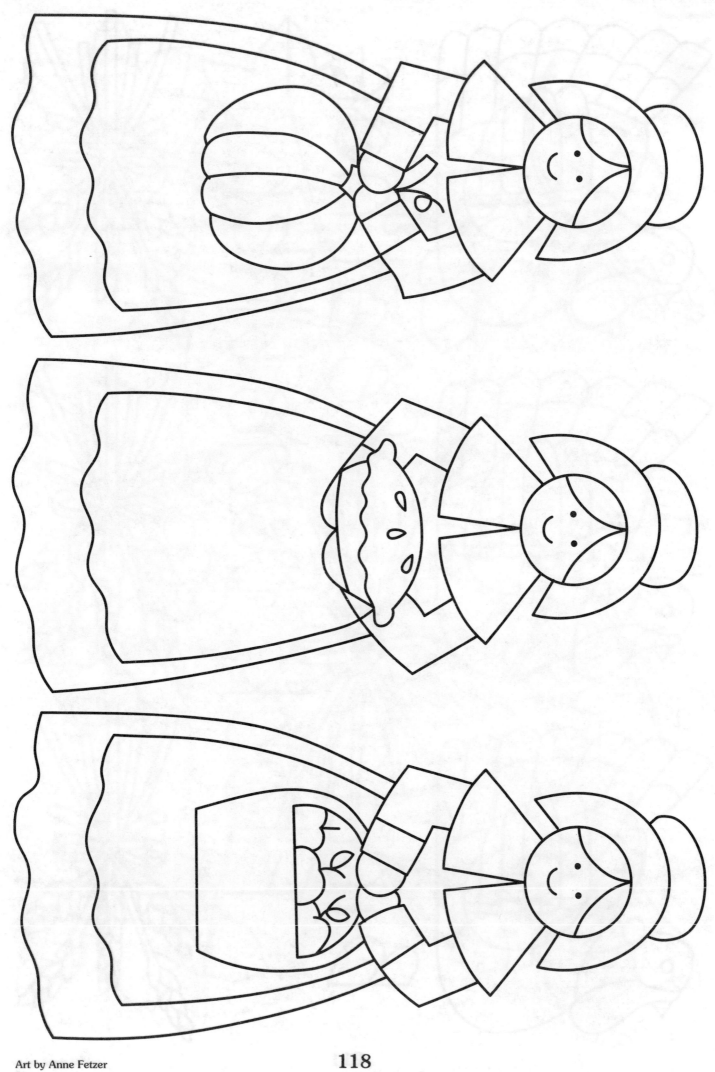

118

Art by Anne Fetzer

AUTUMN
HARVEST

CORN

INDIAN

Art by Anne Feece

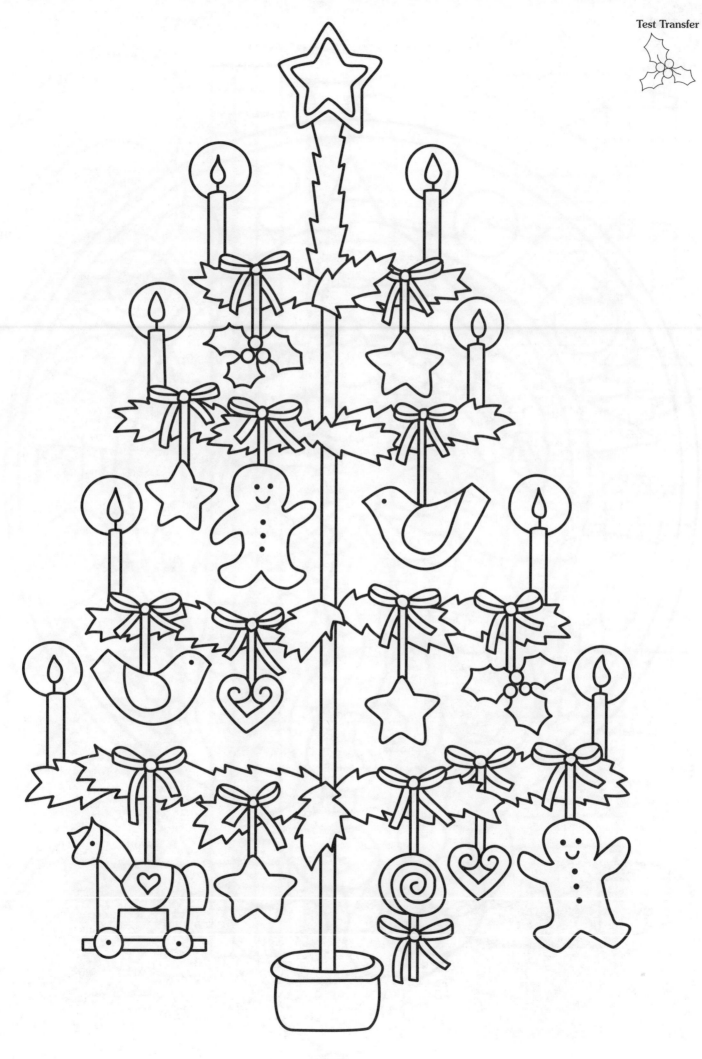

Art by Anne Fetzer

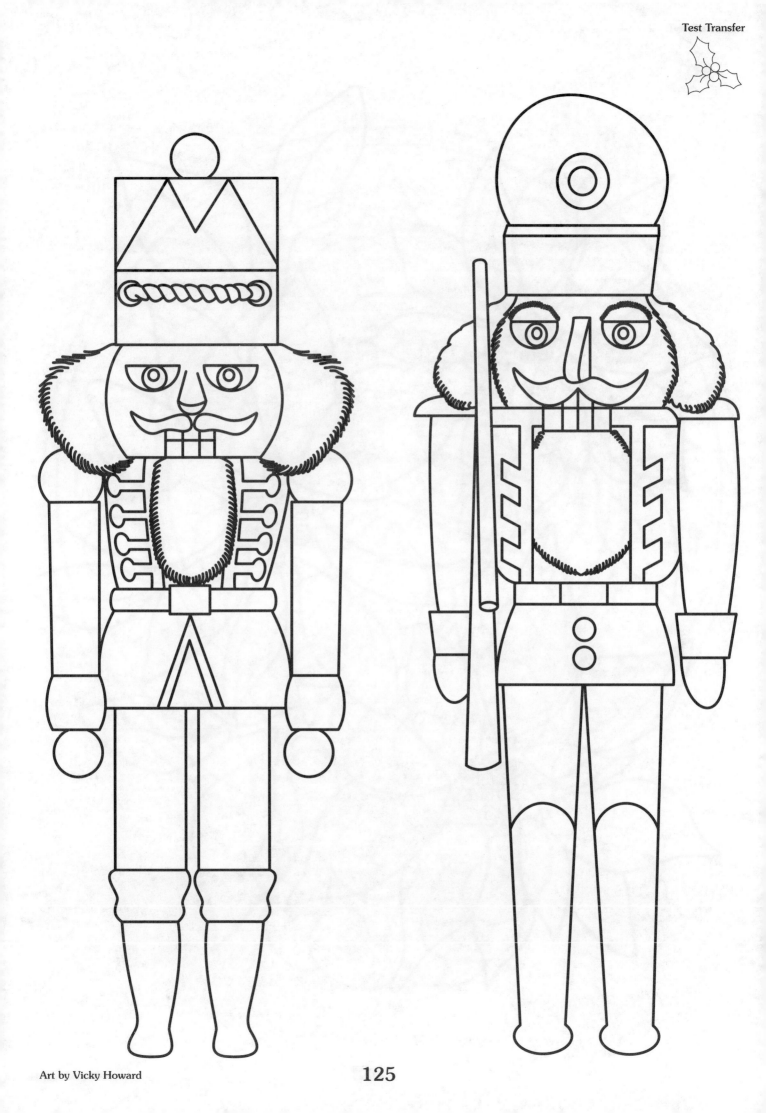

Art by Vicky Howard

125

Art by Vicky Howard

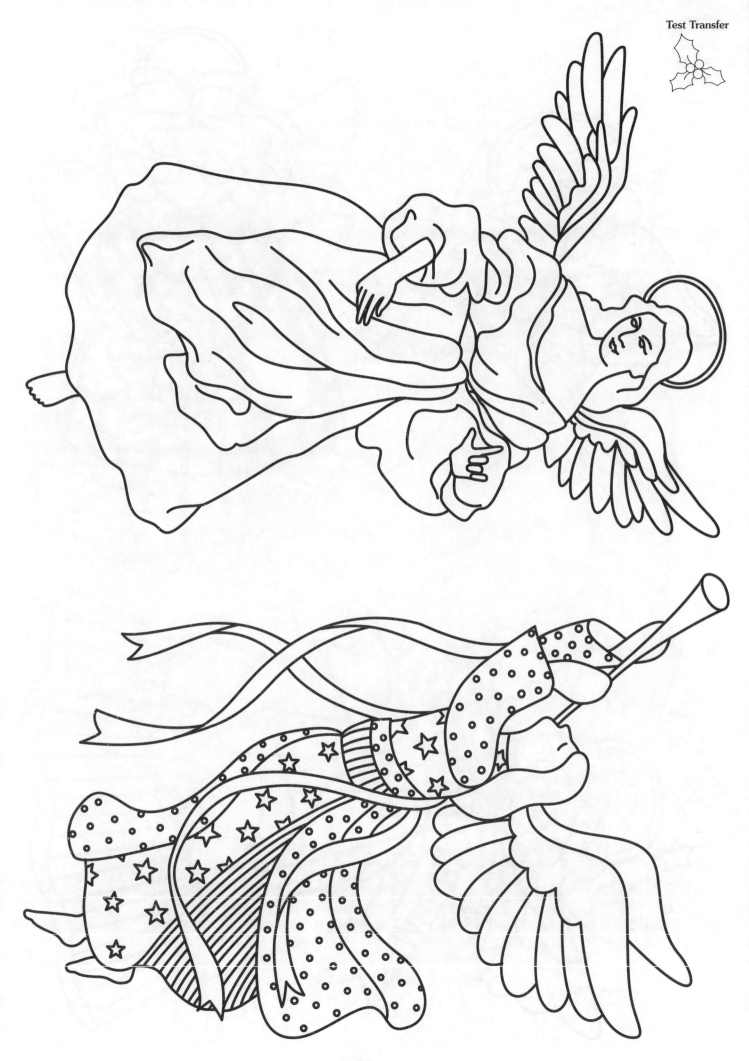

127

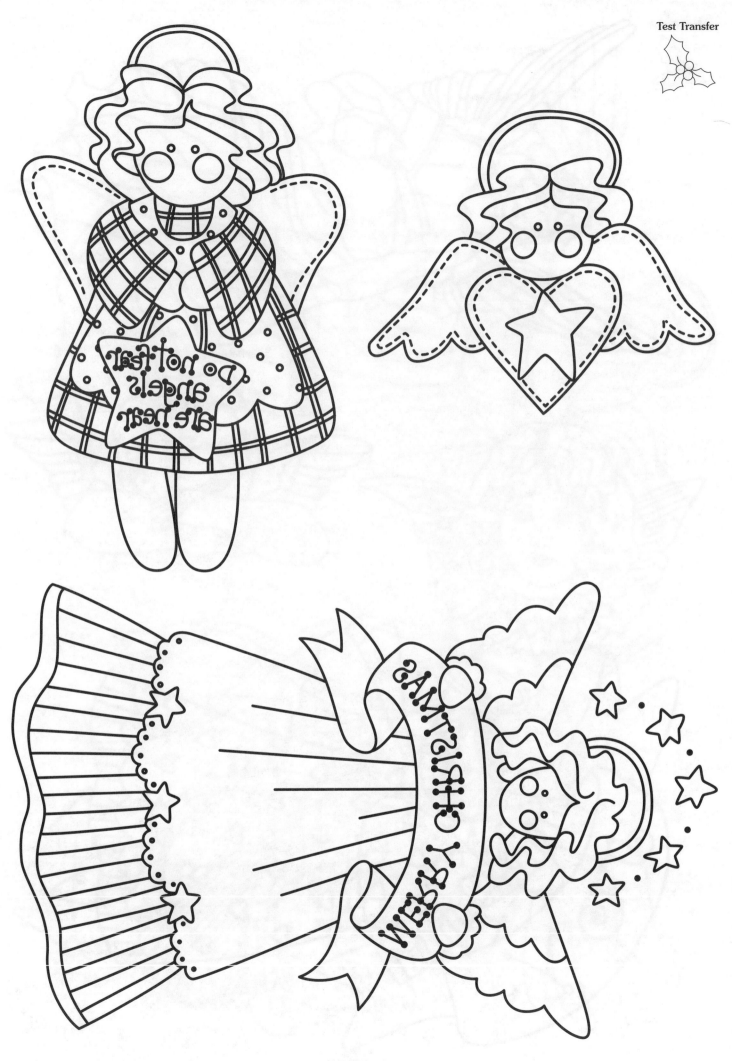

Do not fear
angels
are near

MERRY CHRISTMAS

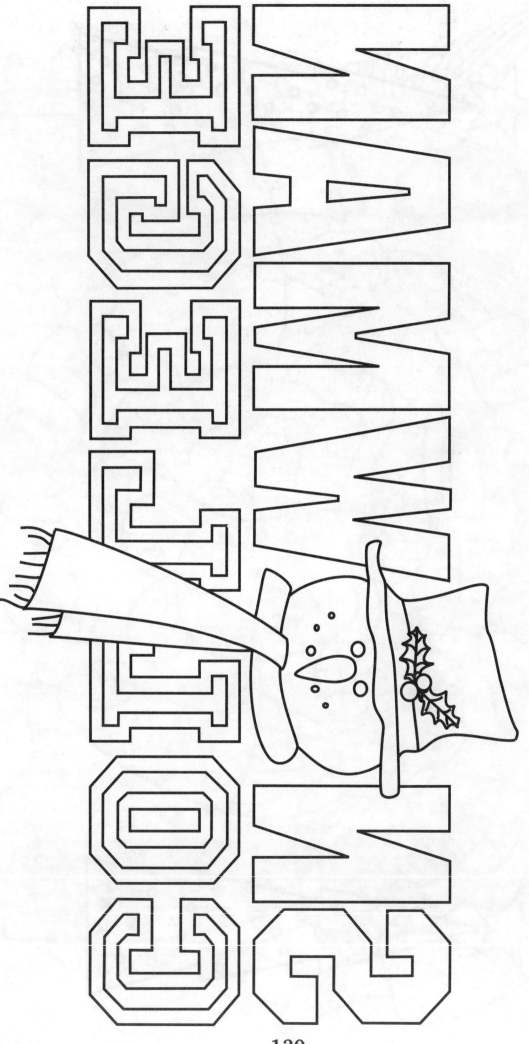

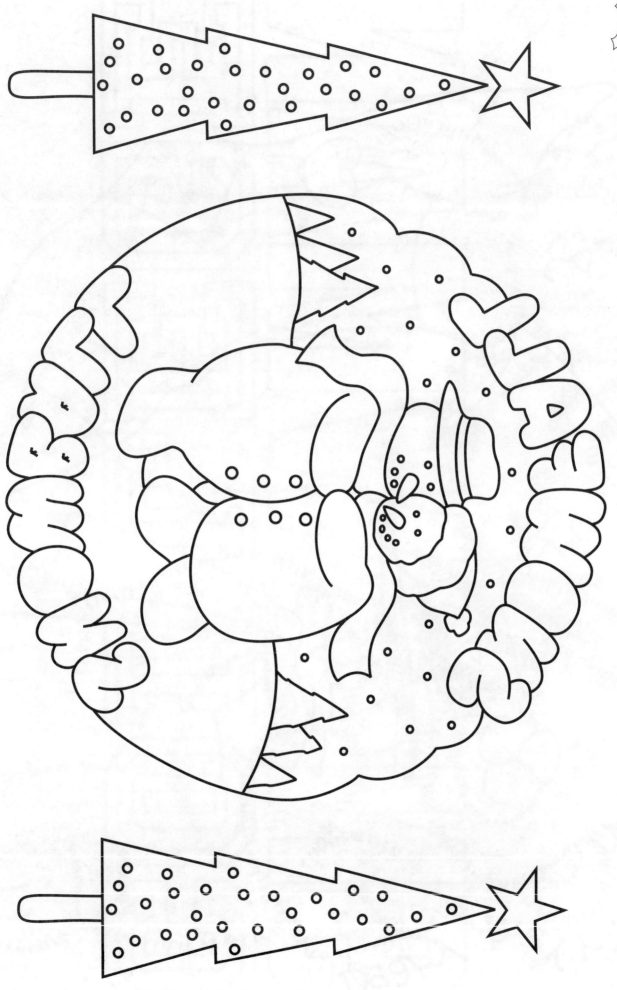

Art by Vicky Howard

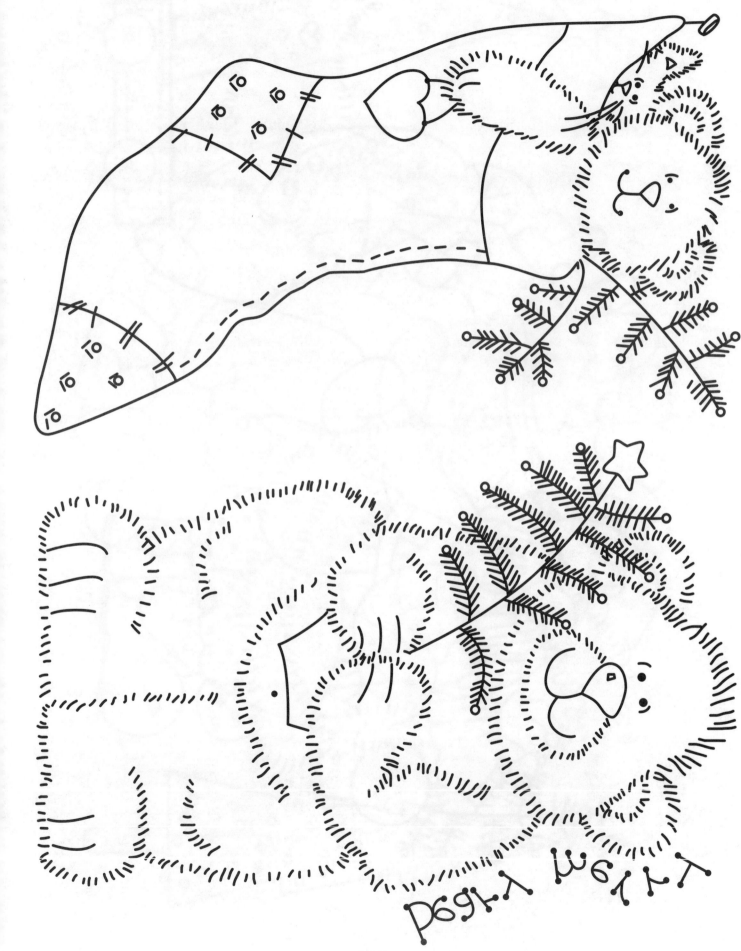

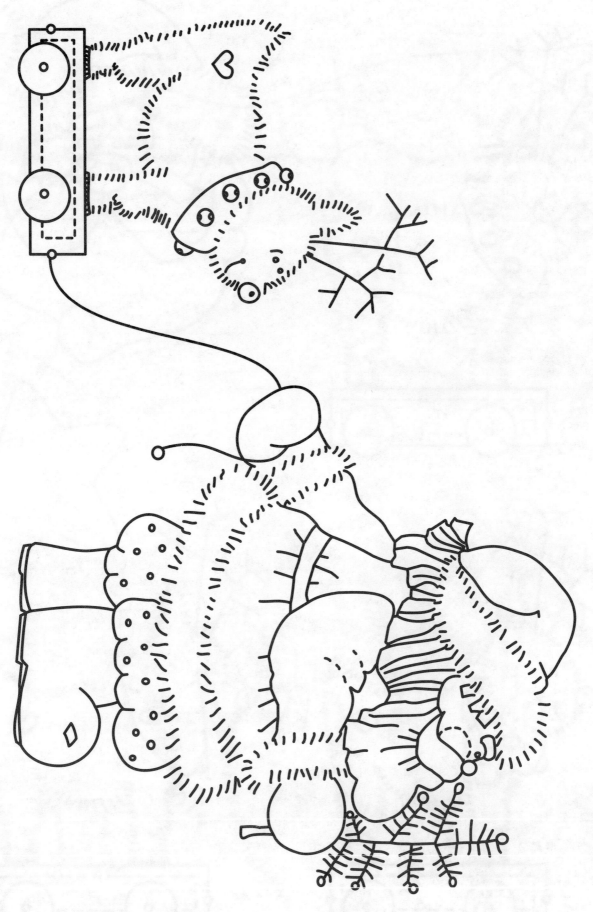

Art by Vicky Howard

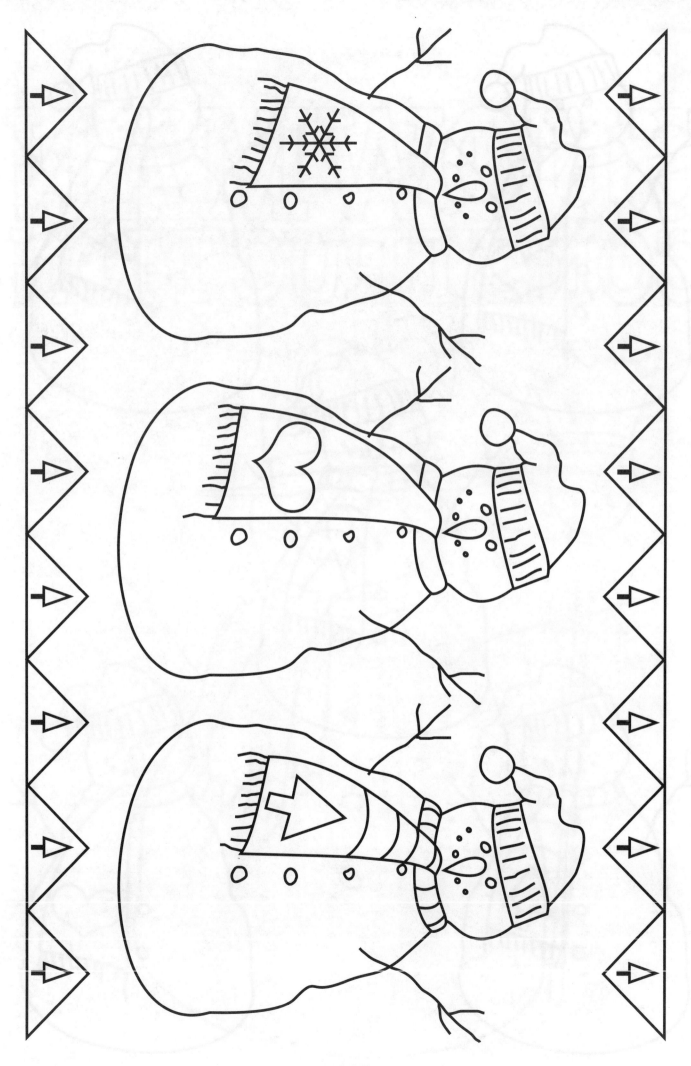

137

Uncle Claus

Art by Kathie Rueger

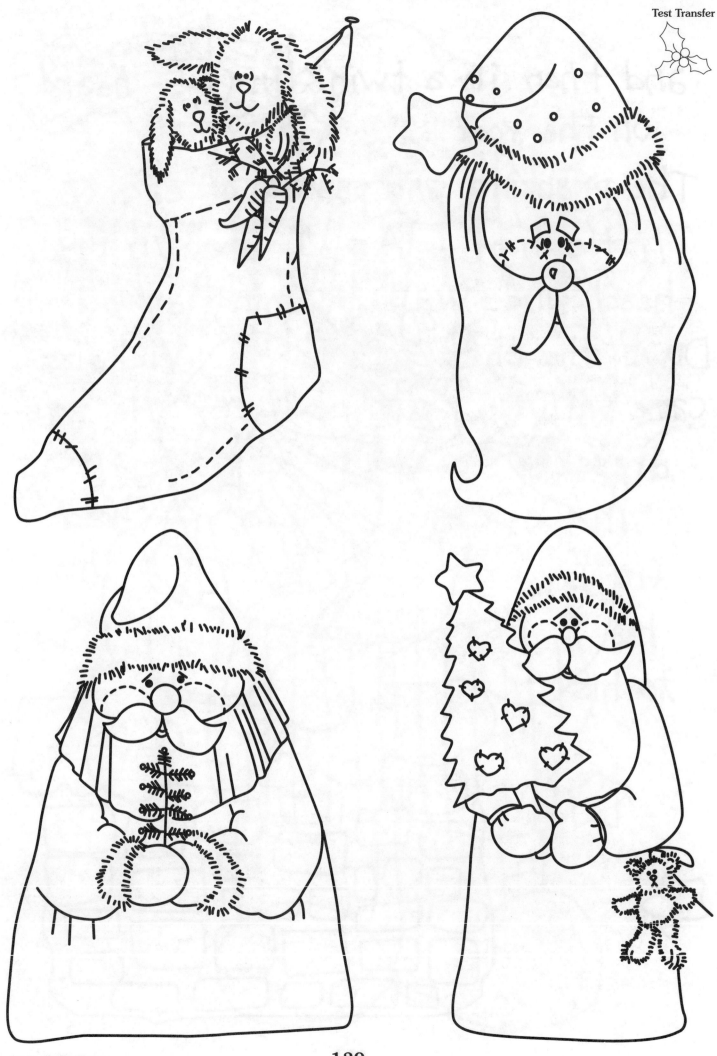

Art by Kathie Rueger

139

and then in a twinkling, I heard
on the roof...
The prancing and pawing of each
little hoof... As I drew in my
head and was turning around,
Down the chimney St. Nicholas
came with a ... He was
dressed all ...

his

to his

and then in a twinkling, I heard
on the roof...

The prancing and pawing of each
little hoof ... As I drew in my
head, and was turning around,
Down the chimney St. Nicholas
came with ... He was
all
dressed
in
fro
hea
to his
red
his

and then in a twinkling, I heard
on the roof...
The prancing and pawing of each
little hoof... As I drew in my
head, and was turning around,
Down the chimney St. Nicholas
came with a bound. He was
dressed all
in
fro   his
hea
to his

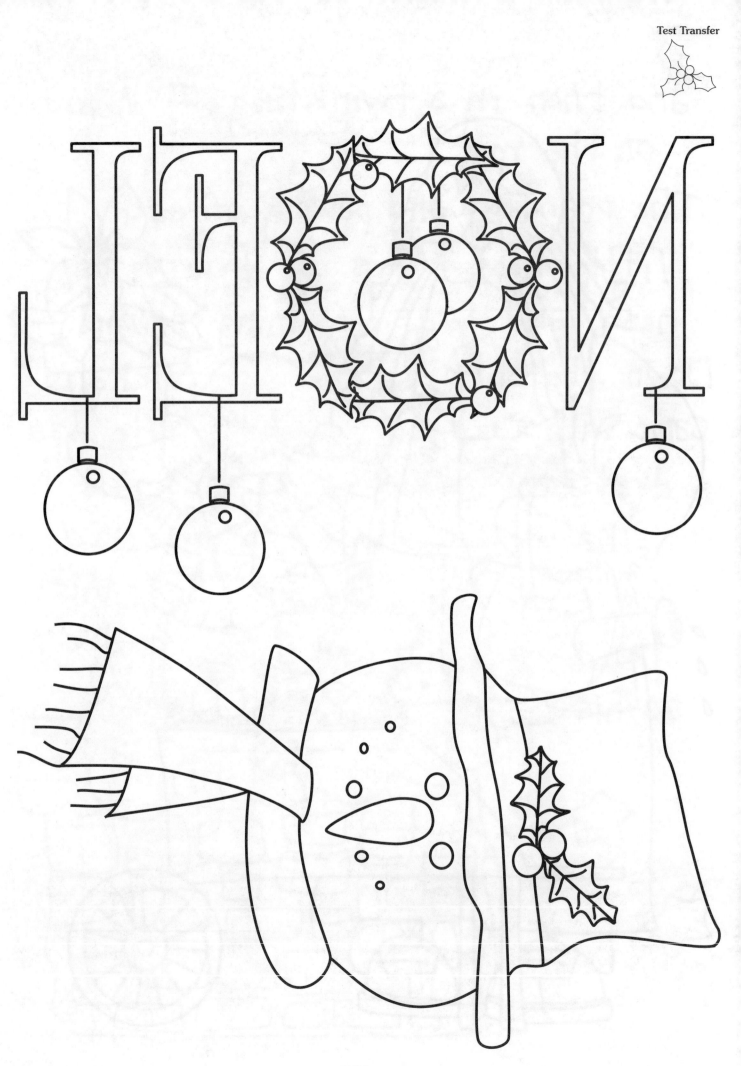

141

SEEDS and TREE

May all your
Christmas wishes
come true!

Art by Kathie Rueger

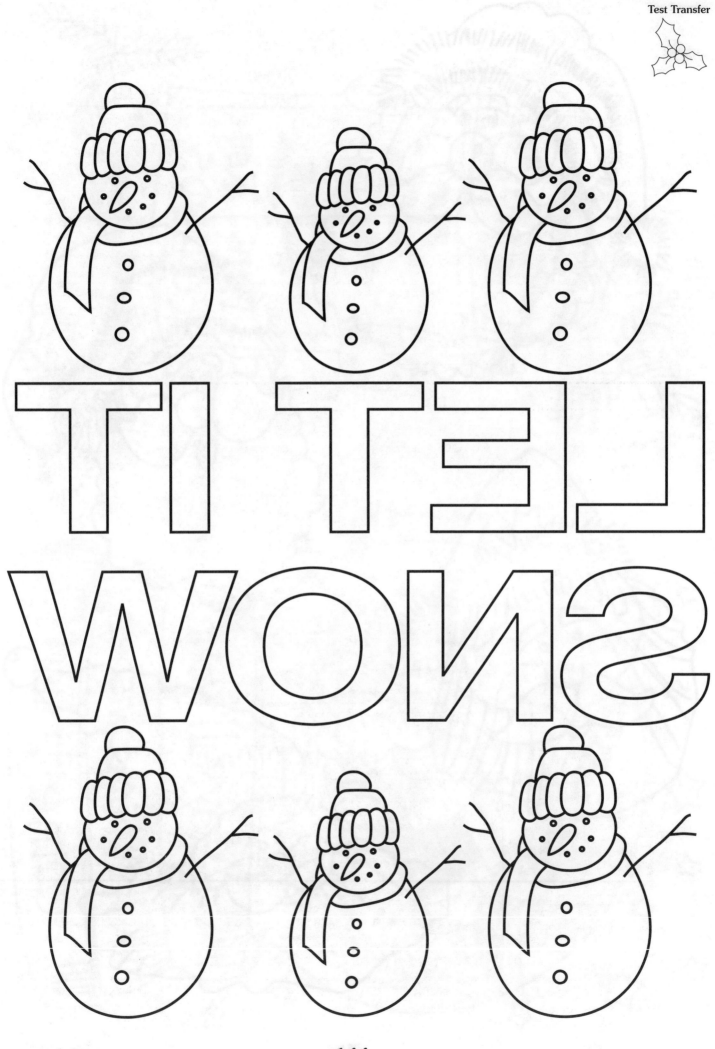

Art by Kathie Rueger

145

Art by Kathie Rueger

146

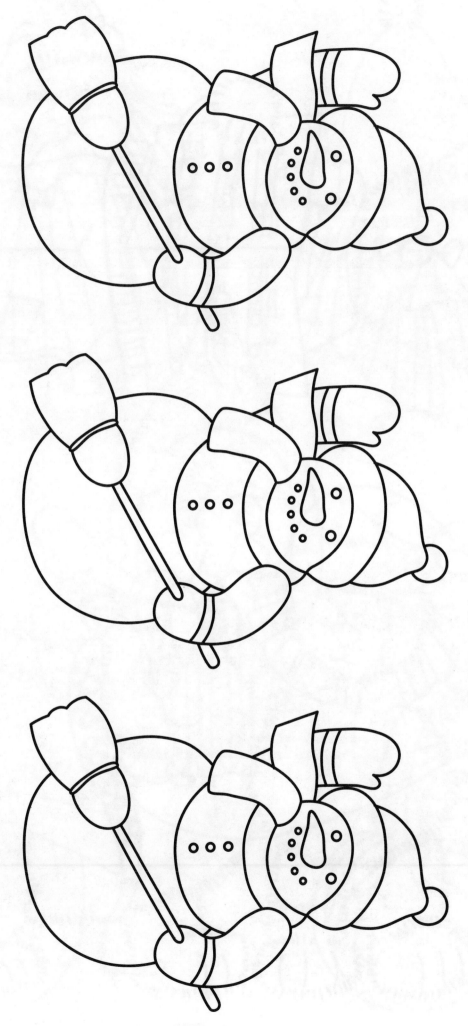

Art by Kathie Rueger

148

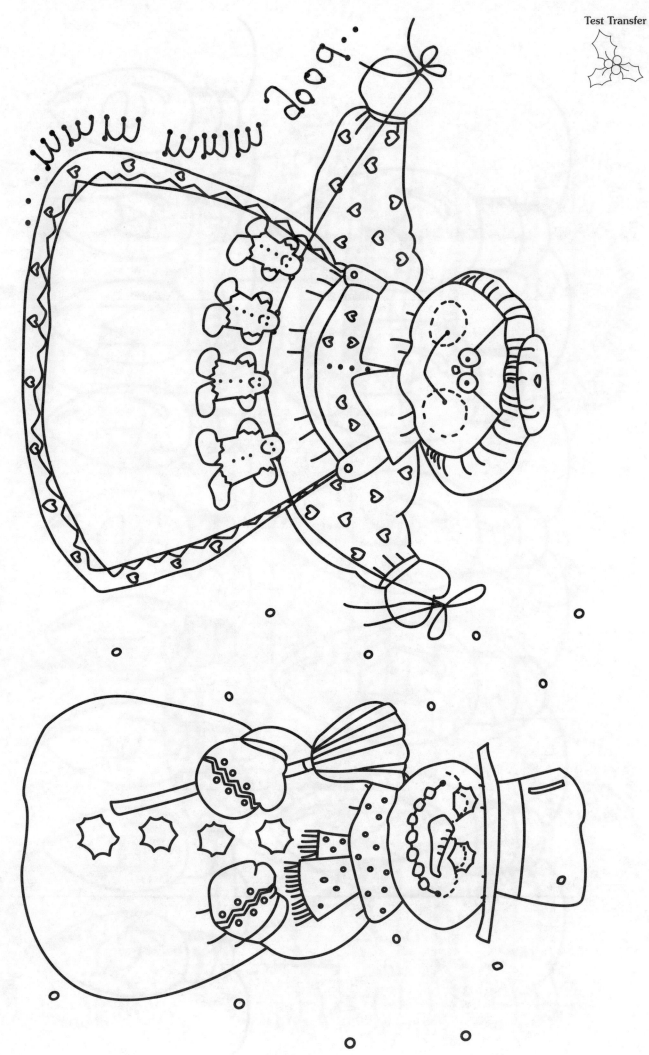

Test Transfer

149

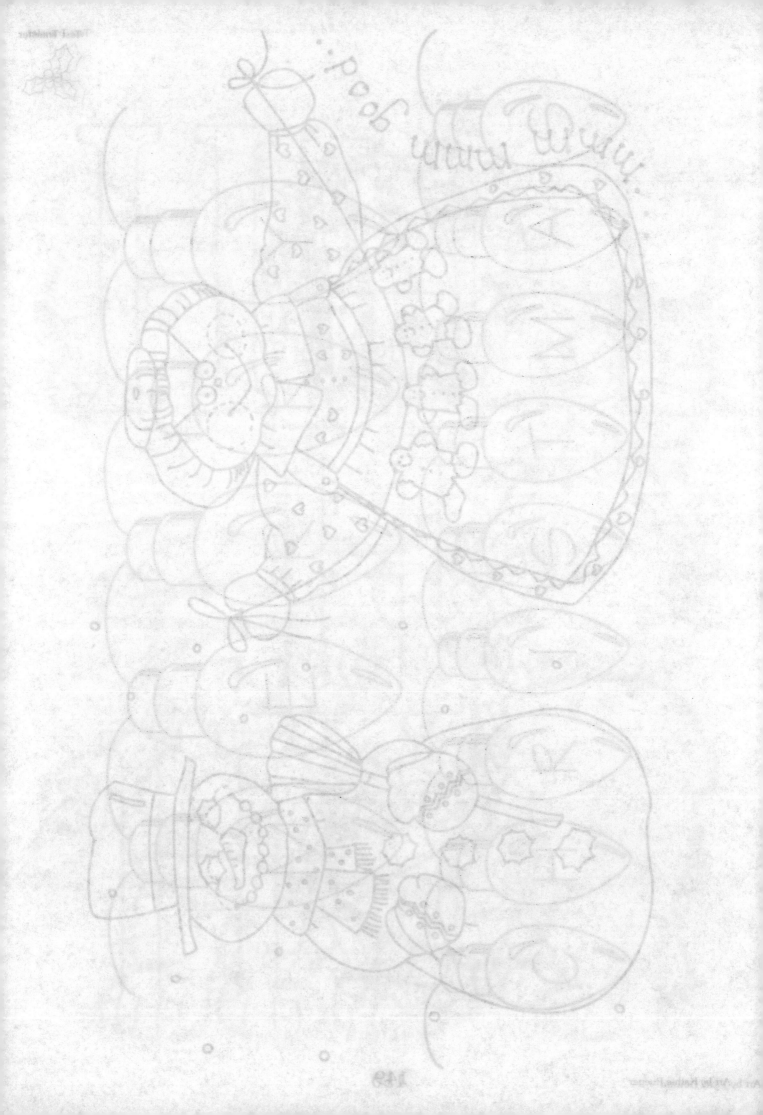

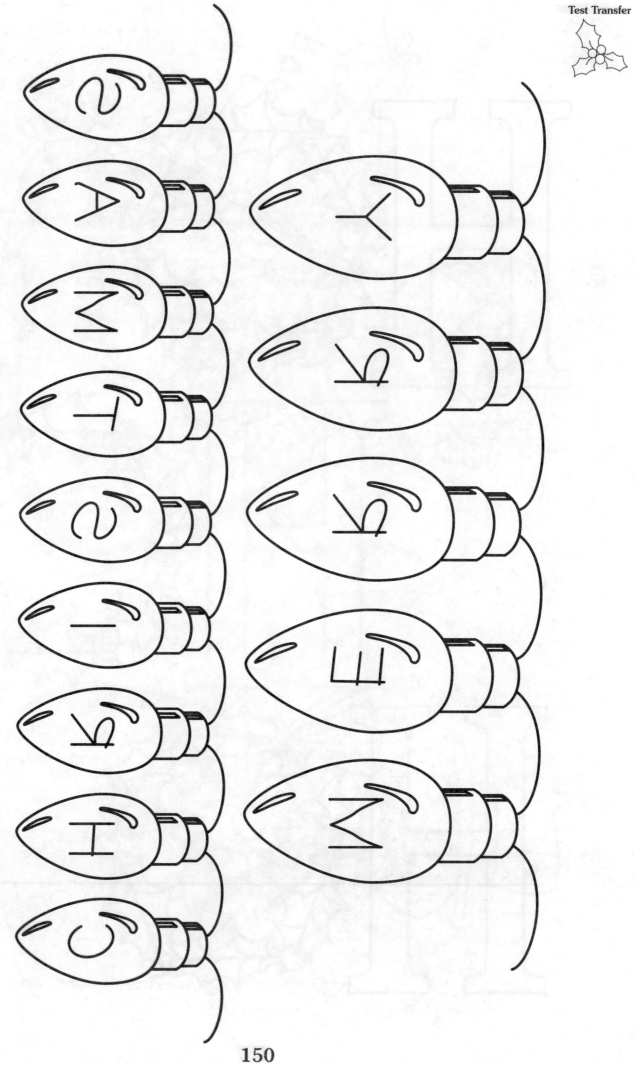

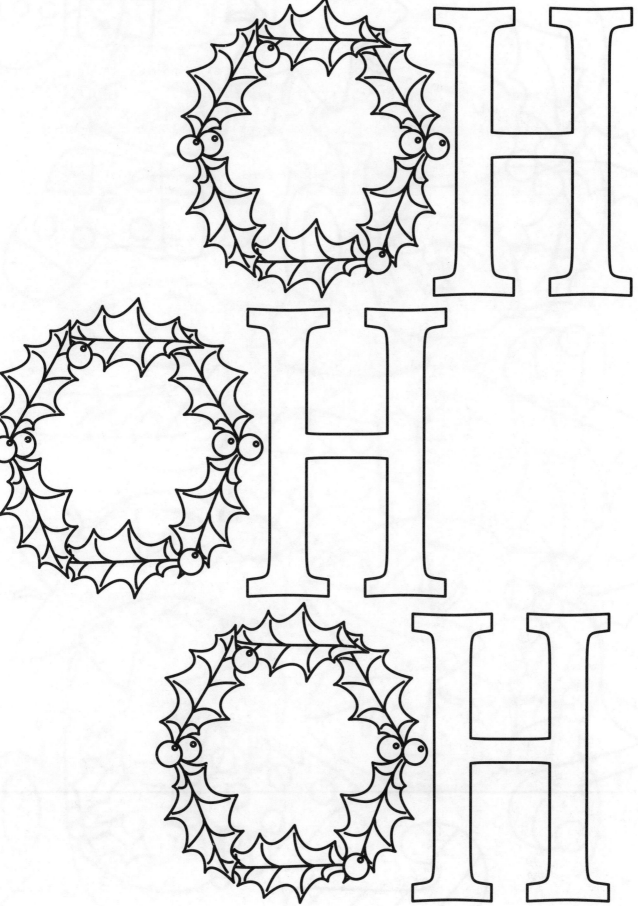

Art by Vicky Howard

Art by Gerri Sorkin

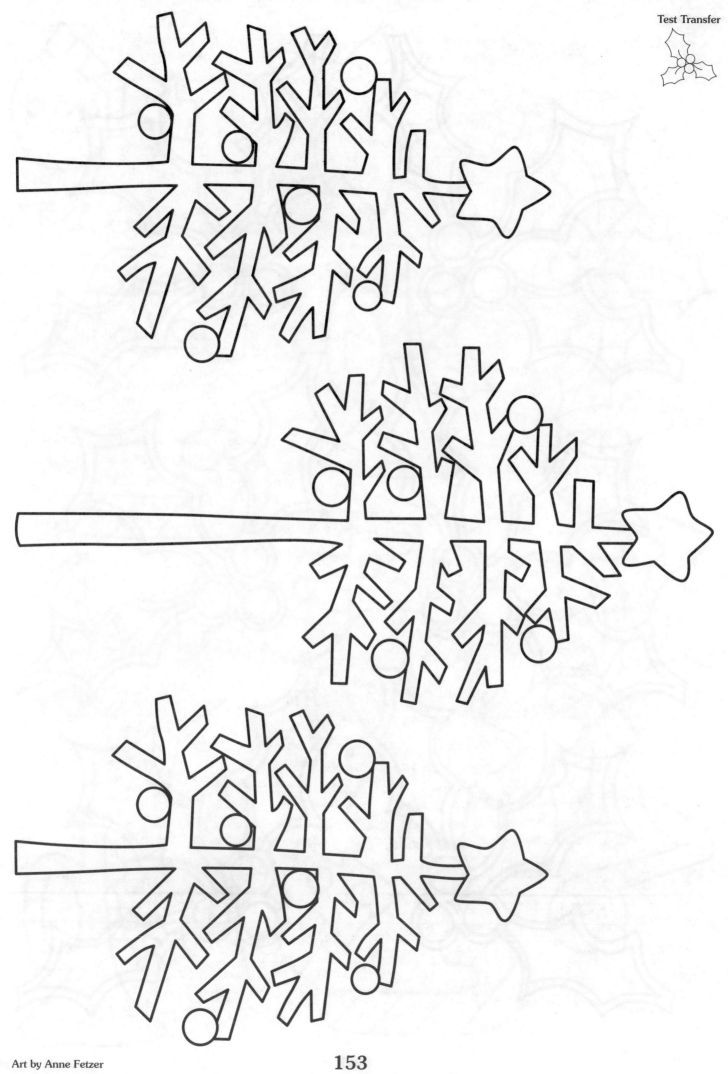

Art by Anne Fetzer

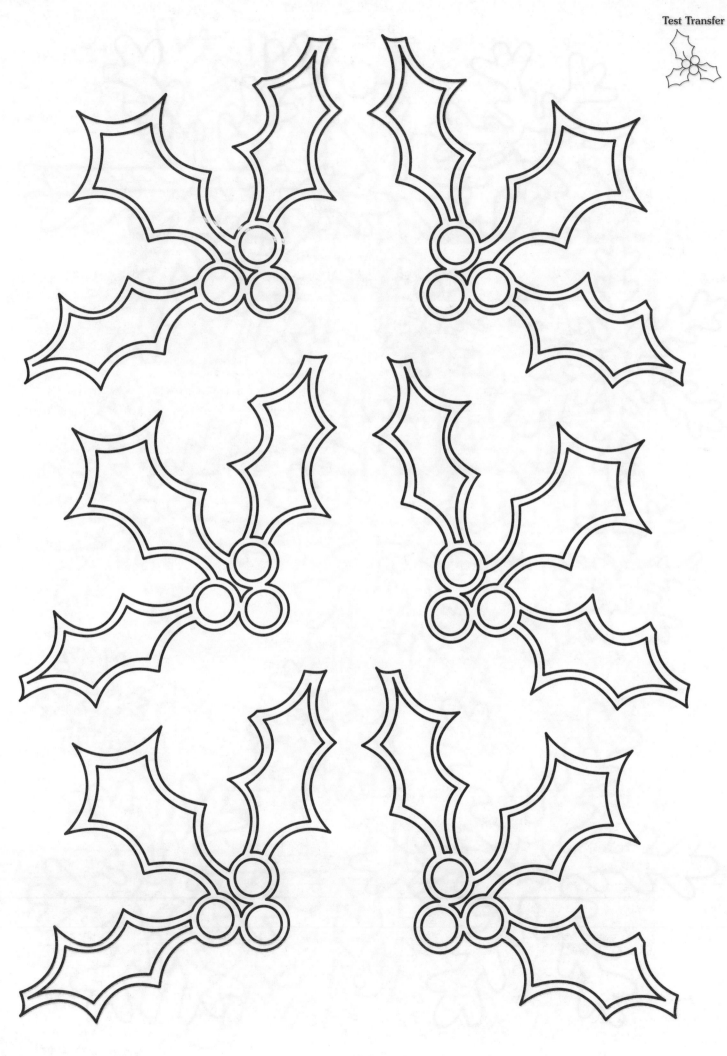

154

155

Art by Anne Fetzer

156

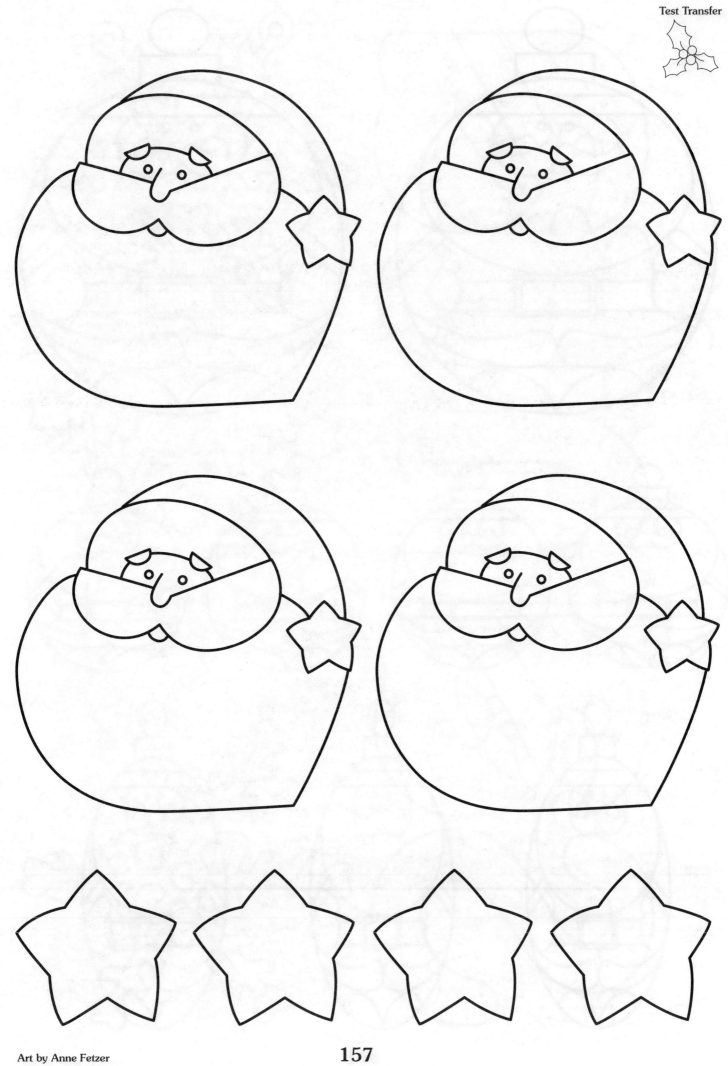

Art by Anne Fetzer

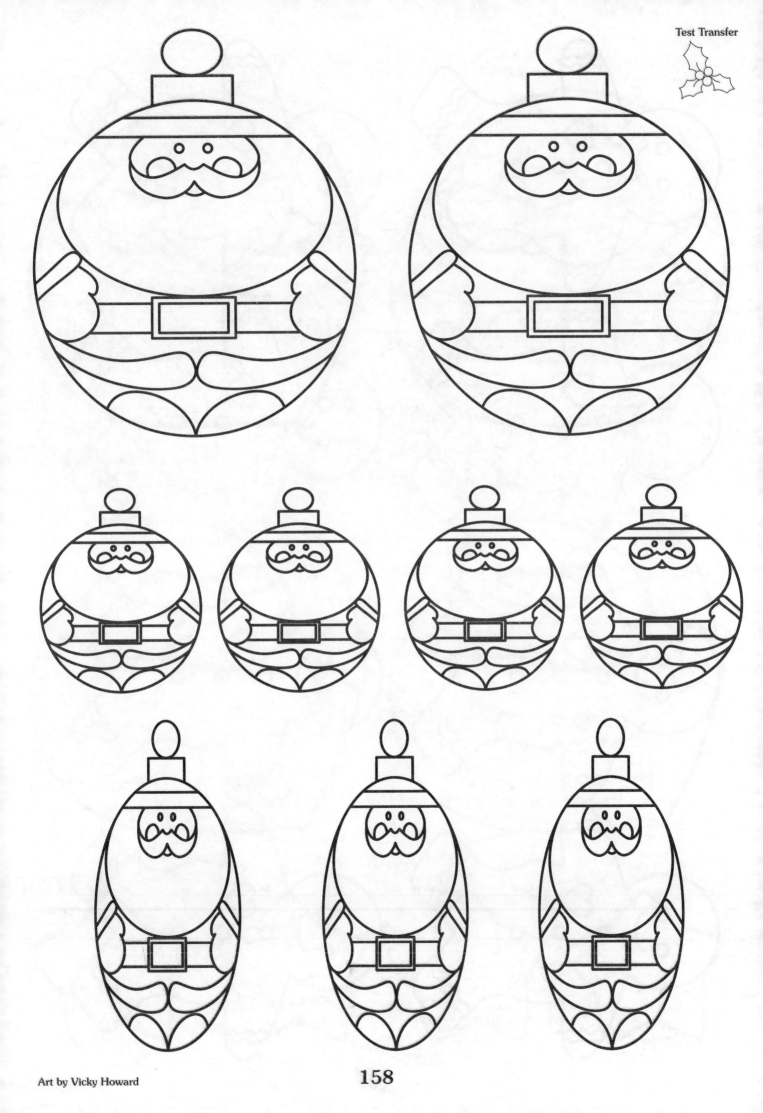

Art by Vicky Howard

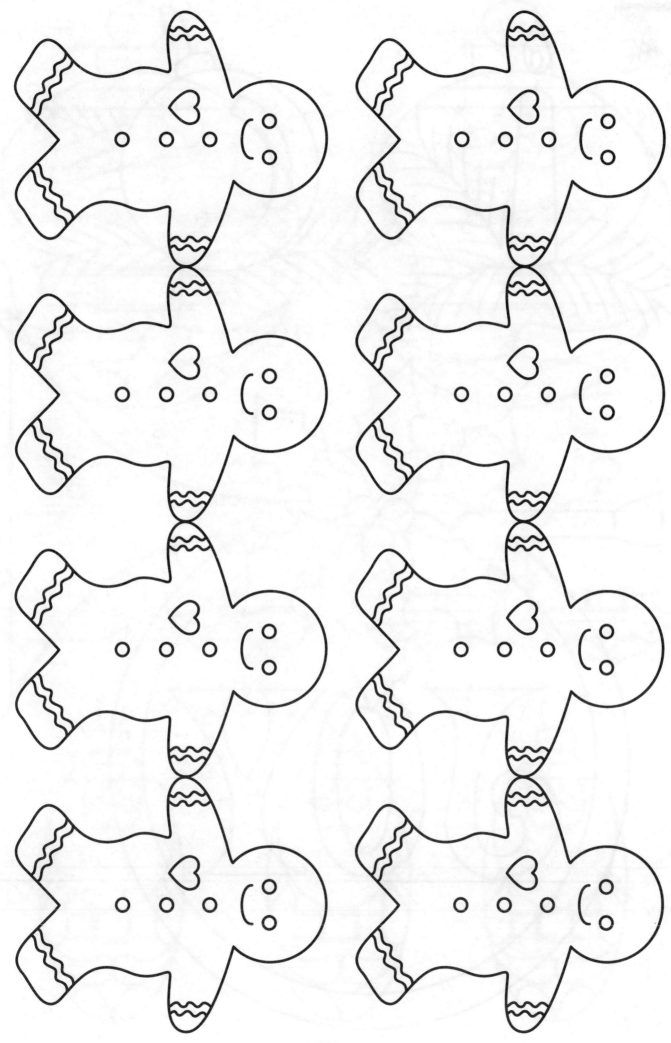

Art by Vicky Howard

Art by Gerri Sorkin

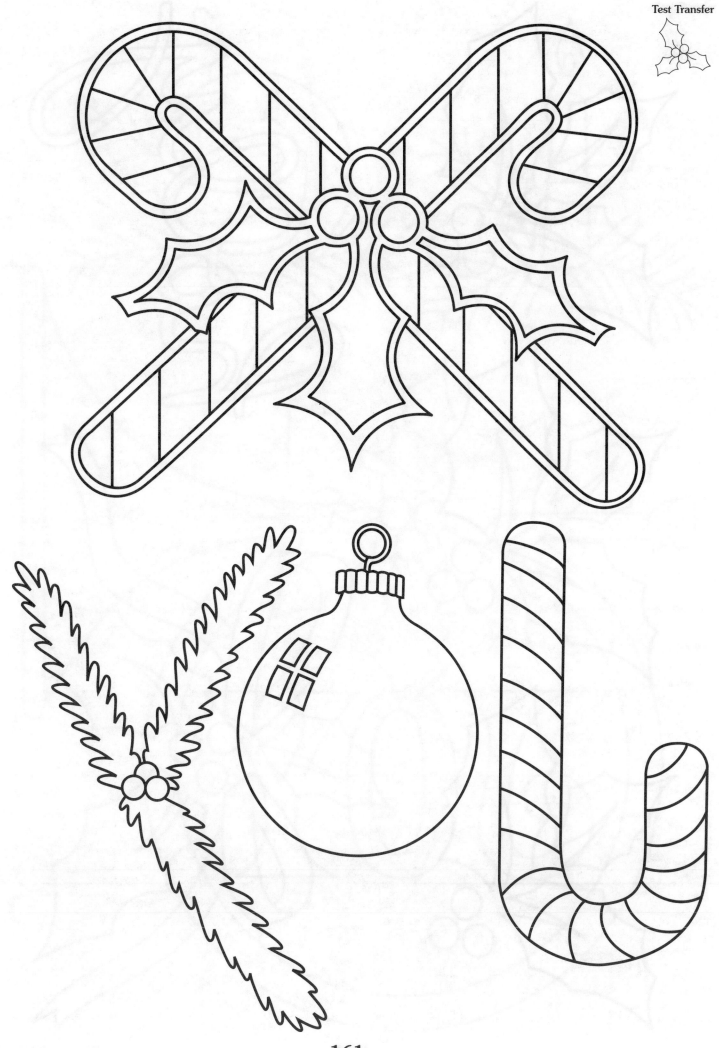

Art by Vicky Howard

161

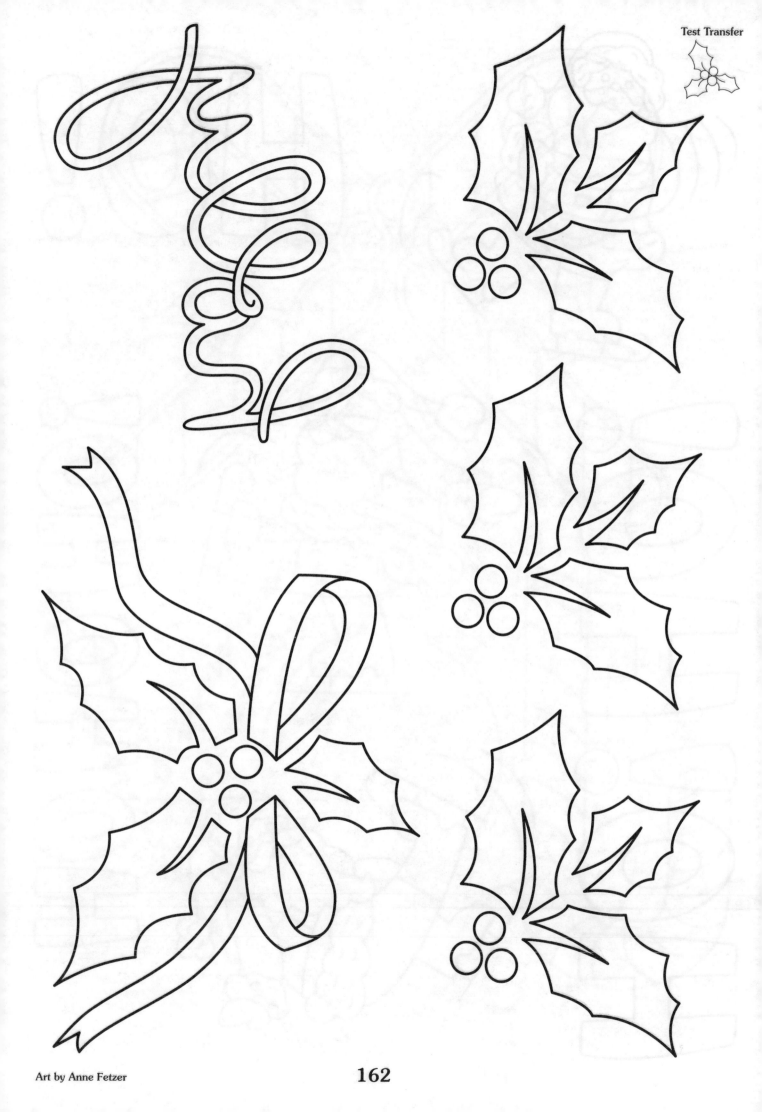

163

Art by Gerri Sorkin

JOY

NOEL

Art by Gerri Sorkin